✝
Sℓ22f

FINGERS

FINGERS

by William Sleator

ATHENEUM 1983 NEW YORK

LIBRARY OF CONGRESS CATALOGING IN PUBLICATION DATA

Sleator, William.   Fingers.

SUMMARY: *Eighteen-year-old Sam falls in with
his mother's bizarre scheme to revitalize his
younger brother's flagging career as a piano
prodigy, and agrees to compose "new works" by a
long dead composer and present them to his brother
as the dictations of a ghost.*
[1. Pianists—Fiction.   2. Brothers—Fiction.
3. Supernatural—Fiction]   I. Title.
PZ7.S6313Fi 1983   [Fic]   83-2662
ISBN 0-689-31000-5

Copyright © 1983 by William Sleator
Published simultaneously in Canada by
McClelland & Stewart, Ltd.
Composition by
Yankee Typesetters, Concord, New Hampshire
Printed and bound by
Fairfield Graphics, Fairfield, Pennsylvania
Designed by Mary Ahern
First Edition

FINGERS

1

"YOU'RE NUTS, Bridget," I said sullenly.

I was stretched out on a bed in a dark little hotel room in Venice, far from the Grand Canal. *Teatro La Fenice*, tomorrow night, was Humphrey's last booking.

"No, I'm not nuts, Sam," Bridget said. "I'd call it imaginative." She was sitting in a rickety chair at the toylike desk in the corner, elegant, even in her bathrobe.

I sighed. "Why don't you just give up and let Humphrey stop performing? You haven't given him a real break in years. It might be good for him. Maybe there's a chance he could still turn out normal."

"That's not the point," said Luc, who was gazing out at the view of a trailer-truck depot. Luc is Bridget's second husband, to whom she is unfortunately still married, and he was not elegant at all in *his* bathrobe, dark stubble on his face, his legs like flabby toadstools. Naturally he didn't want Humphrey, his main claim to fame, to stop performing. But he still couldn't stomach Bridget's plan. "The point is that it's too dangerous. It just won't work."

"It all depends on what you mean by 'work'," Bridget said, lighting a cigarette. As usual, her red hair was tightly braided and done up into a bun at the back of her head, her pale face carefully made up. She never tells her age, but I'm eighteen and she's my mother, so she's probably at least forty. She still looks young, though, and on that day she seemed almost girlish. "No, I don't expect musicologists will be clamoring to write learned articles about Humphrey. I don't even expect the *critics* to be instantly convinced, cretinous though they are. But I can promise you that Humphrey will get publicity, oodles of it. And that will lead to bookings. Maybe not first class concert circuit, but . . ." She shrugged and smiled. "But we're not exactly in a position to be choosy, are we?"

We weren't. For ten years we had all depended on Humphrey. And now at fifteen, Humphrey was washed up.

HUMPHREY is my half-brother, Luc's son. His career started with a bang when, at the age of five, he did the Mozart A Major with the Cleveland Symphony. God knows how Bridget even got him in the door, God knows how she convinced them that it would not be a total fiasco; I was only eight at the time and don't remember the details. But from the moment that tiny little kid teetered over to the thirteen-foot Bösendorfer Grand, clambered up onto the bench, and then ripped into the opening passages, he had the audience in the palm of his hand.

And they were big hands too, even then. Not like my puny little appendages. Sure, I had had piano lessons. Bridget was a music nut, especially after she got

4

hooked up with Luc, a defunct prodigy himself. I didn't really go for Luc, but the lessons were wonderful, because I loved music, at the beginning. I loved the clean mathematical aspect of harmony, the interplay between chords, the satisfying logic of it. The only trouble was, I couldn't play. Partly it was my small hands, which even now won't span an octave. And partly it was my general clumsiness, a total lack of mechanical skill. I knew what the music was supposed to sound like, but I couldn't get the message through to my fingers. They flopped around on the keyboard like beached minnows, refusing to obey.

Humphrey barely weighed four pounds when he was born, and he stayed small all through his childhood. He just happened to have enormous hands and feet, as disproportionately large as mine were small. He had a lot more trouble learning to read music than I did. I can still remember his little wordless, hopeless whimperings of protest—they started on him before he could even talk. But once they had drilled the notes into him by rote and those fingers took over, then he could do anything.

"Sammy! Leave Humphrey alone!" Bridget would yell at me twenty times a day. Luc didn't yell; he just pushed me away from Humphrey with *his* big hairy hands. But I couldn't think of one reason why I shouldn't pick on the little brat. Not only was he ugly and noisy and backward (he wore smelly diapers until he was five), he also had a real father. What was especially humiliating was that he was so good at something I loved and couldn't do. And so as soon as Humphrey began to play well, I lost all interest in the piano. And neither Bridget nor Luc tried to rekindle it in me; now that they had Humphrey, they couldn't care less whether I played or not. I haven't touched the instrument since I was six.

I would have avoided music altogether, but it was impossible in that house, with Humphrey practicing all the time. I'd get as far away as I could and close all the doors and bury myself in books about dinosaurs and history and geology and math—anything that was real, that had hard facts. But the music still came through. There was no way I couldn't hear it. And the logic of it made more and more sense to me. Against my will, my understanding of the relationships between the chords grew more vivid, just from having to listen to Humphrey all the time. But even though I understood it, I was still able to hate it. I hated music; I hated the piano; I hated Humphrey; I hated everything.

After the Cleveland concert, and another one in Chicago, Humphrey began to be a celebrity. That was not too long after World War II, and people were ready for a phenomenon like Humphrey. Now, not only did he have music, and Bridget, and a father, he also had the love and adoration of the whole world. That's how it looked to me at the time, anyway. The pain was bad at first. I tortured Humphrey unmercifully; I made terrible screaming scenes. Once I kicked a photographer in the shin and then knocked the camera out of his hands, breaking the lens—that was the only time Bridget ever hit me (after the photographers had all gone away, of course).

Still, I wasn't a fool. It didn't take me long to notice that the tantrums and scenes, even the rich voluptuous pleasure of making Humphrey howl, in the end only made me feel bleaker. I fought and struggled and finally succeeded in becoming numb. I would be indifferent to the idiotic brouhaha the world made over Humphrey, indifferent to the triviality of music and the arts. I would be above it all, aloof.

This attitude made life pleasanter for everyone, including myself. It was practical too, because if I'd gone on being a nuisance they would have sent me away, and I would not have been able to enjoy the benefits of Humphrey's phenomenal success. "Enjoy" is too positive a word; but I did derive a cold satisfaction from the travels to foreign countries, the hotels and restaurants, the private tutor, the boat trips—all provided by Humphrey's career. As for Humphrey himself, I made a continuous effort to avoid looking at him, speaking to him, listening to him. He was not a little boy, he was a *thing*; and the only safe and sane way to deal with this object was to feel nothing about it at all.

Tiny darling Humphrey, with his cute little outfits, his baby face, his carefully styled bangs. At the age of seven he looked like a five year old; at ten he looked seven; at thirteen, Bridget was still pushing him out on stage in short pants, and he could pass for eight. Of course Humphrey had no understanding of the music he memorized so dutifully, no expression or interpretation. His popularity depended solely on the bizarre novelty of watching an infant, dwarfed by his instrument, bang out those great crashing chords, those lightning arpeggios. Even the most hostile and acerbic critics couldn't resist comparing him to the young Mozart.

And then, three months after Humphrey hit fourteen, adolescence pounced, with vengeance. Humphrey began to grow.

There's a Greek legend about a king named Procrustes, who had a special bed in his house upon which all travelers through his domain were forced to lie. Procrustes wanted everyone to be the right size for this bed. If the unhappy traveler was too short for it, Procrustes had him stretched on a rack until he was long enough. If he was too tall, Procrustes would chop off his feet and whatever amount of leg was necessary to enable his guest to fit comfortably in bed. Bridget was aware that using such methods on Humphrey would be considered inappropriate. Though it does seem odd that she didn't at least try hormones. At any rate, for once Bridget was faced with a situation she could not control. All she could do was sit back helplessly and watch Humphrey grow.

It all happened at once. One day I could easily have lifted him by the nape of his neck; the next day, I had to look up to stick my tongue out at him. I had experienced adolescence at the age of thirteen, and never got taller than five feet eight. Humphrey passed six feet and kept right on going. He developed a great deal of soft bulk around his middle and on his upper arms and thighs. His voice deepened. Dark hair sprouted on his face and legs and hands. At fourteen he could pass for eighteen; at fifteen, he looked twenty.

I had trained myself so rigidly to suppress feelings that I almost couldn't enjoy watching Humphrey's career topple. I was amused, like a vaguely interested bystander watching a demolished building collapse to the ground.

Bridget was the helpless victim trapped on the top

floor. She didn't scream for help or have hysterics or fall to pieces; she's too self-controlled for that. At first she tried to brazen it out and pressure people into booking him anyway. But the audiences stopped coming. When he was an adorable toddler, it hadn't mattered that Humphrey didn't know *piano* from *forte*; it did matter, however, when he became a big, unattractive man pounding woodenly at the keyboard. Bridget forced Luc to try to teach Humphrey something about musicianship, now that it seemed necessary. But Humphrey was unable to absorb it; and since Luc's performing career had ended at about the same age, he didn't have much to teach. Bridget grew more silent and tense and withdrawn as the bookings dissolved and the income dwindled. She stopped talking to Luc. She began to look old.

BUT on that day in the tiny hotel room in Venice, she seemed her old self again as she described her crackpot plan. I really did think at first that she had gone crazy. For a minute I almost felt sorry for her. I should have known better.

"Humphrey," she said, "will be visited by the ghost of a dead composer. This composer will dictate pieces of music to Humphrey—in his own characteristic style, of course." She lit a cigarette. "They need only be short little pieces. Humphrey can introduce the first one as an encore."

"If he gets enough applause for an encore," I put in.

She ignored me. "We can still afford to be subtle. There will probably be some knowledgeable critics at this next concert. All Humphrey needs to do is announce a piece that doesn't exist by this famous composer. It will cause quite a stir." She blew out smoke. "When they interview Humphrey afterward, he can explain how the music was dictated to him."

Luc and I, in agreement for once, made our objections. Bridget mentioned publicity and bookings. "We're not exactly in a position to be choosy, are we?" she said.

"But the timing will make it so transparent," argued Luc, turning from the window and running a hand through his graying mop of dark hair. "To introduce this spirit communication just when his popularity is at its lowest ebb. It's an obvious bid for attention. They'll see right through us."

"Us?" said Bridget, pressing her carefully manicured hand to her thin chest. "I didn't say anything about *us*. It will all come from Humphrey. *We* will be just as skeptical as everyone else. But Humphrey will believe. I think he will be quite convincing when he explains it in that simple way of his."

"And we all know how simple Humphrey is," I said.

"I resent that," Luc said mildly.

"We all know how simple Humphrey is," I repeated, just to rub it in. "But even *he* doesn't believe in Santa Claus any more. Just give up and let him have a normal life. How do you expect to get him to believe in this ghost, anyway?"

"As usual, the simplest way is the best," she said. "We will just use a little chemical help. Humphrey's never taken a sleeping pill in his life. A three-quarter grain Seconal should do the trick. Slip it to him at dinner, and in an hour he'll be out like a light—and he will *not* remember what happened just before he passed out.

That's how barbiturates work. There will be a blank in his memory when he wakes up. And if he wakes up at a desk with a pen in his hand and a hastily scrawled composition beside it—with the ink still wet, as they say—the conclusion will be obvious. Especially if we fill in a few details, telling him how he worked feverishly all night, mumbling foreign words, conversing with an unseen presence. He'll be convinced."

Luc had removed his glasses and was gazing at her, his lips slightly parted. "You know, there's a chance that you have something there," he admitted, beginning to be won over. "But do we have to drug him? I find that a little distasteful."

"Distasteful?" I snorted. "You didn't find it distasteful to chain him to the piano bench for eight hours a day when he was two. So what's a little medicine?"

"Shut up, Sam," Bridget said, her attention still on Luc. "It's a tiny dose, darling. It won't do him any harm. He's a big boy, you know."

"Well, maybe," Luc said, nodding slowly. "Maybe you do have something . . ."

"Except for one little detail," I said, still reclining on the bed. "Where are you going to dig up this music from beyond the grave? It has to be music no one's heard before. It has to be convincing. Just where do you think it's going to come from?"

Bridget tilted her head to the side and smiled, directing her charm in my direction now. "But Sammy, dear, you've always had a marvelous ear. It wouldn't be any trouble at all for you to dash something off."

"*Me?*" The bedsprings whined in B flat as I bounced

to my feet. I thought I was furious, so I snapped at her. "You expect *me* to write these fake compositions? I've never composed anything in my life!"

Luc cleared his throat. "Don't you think that *I*, as the professional, would do better?" he said. "Sam's a musical failure."

"You can check the music over, Luc," Bridget said, dismissing him, still fixing me with her pale glittering eye. "But Sammy, you cannot pretend you don't understand music. I know you. I've seen the way you listen. I've seen the way you look at scores. You couldn't hit the notes, but you always knew the chords, even when you were a baby."

I was flattered that she wanted me instead of Luc. And perhaps it was not anger that was making my pulse pick up. Perhaps it was a new kind of excitement, a feeling I had forgotten about. I was good at something. I was needed.

But I didn't know how to accept it. I wasn't prepared. I only knew how to be ornery. "Even if I could do it, who says I want to?" I said sourly. "It's hard to compose music. It would be easier to let Humphrey stop performing, and better for him. Why should I go to all that trouble just to save his dumb career?"

"His dumb career?" Bridget sounded baffled, but at least she was finally allowing herself to hear and acknowledge the idea I'd been pushing more and more over the last few months. "Stop performing? Sammy, do you know what you're saying?"

"Uh . . . sure," I said uncomfortably. "It's just not working any more. It's awful for Humphrey, the way you push him out there to be ridiculed. He'd be better off at home. We all would."

"You're not making sense, Sam," she said. "How could we *think* of giving up now, when he's just beginning to mature, to learn what it means to be a real artist? Performing is what he's *meant* for, Sam. I couldn't take that away from him. It would be like depriving him of . . . of food, or shelter. How could I do that to my own baby?"

I winced. There it was again, the intolerable fact that I was always trying to avoid, but couldn't. Bridget loved Humphrey more than anything in the world—more than she loved Luc, more than she loved me. She loved him so much she was kind of warped by it, compelled to make the whole world love him too—even if she had to drug him and lie to him to do it. That was what love meant to Bridget.

"But couldn't he learn to be an artist by staying home and studying in peace and not performing again until he gets good?" I said rather hopelessly. "We could get by without the money he makes."

That was true. Luc's family had money, and enough of it came our way so that we could survive, barely—but survive. That was why Bridget had married him, of course. Her marriage to my impractical and headstrong father had been an immature fling, a romantic mistake that hadn't worked. He had deserted us. It had left her determined to find someone who would not only give her security, but would allow himself to be pushed around—someone like Luc. Bridget liked money, and she liked being in charge.

But it hadn't been very wise of me to mention money: I think there was a part of her that resented me for the hardship she had suffered with my father. Her jawbone tightened under the stretched skin as she stood up. Her eyes went on glittering, but her voice turned to ice. "You dare to mention money, Sam?" she said softly. "After being supported so lavishly all these years, while you lazed around doing nothing? Don't you think it's about time you made a contribution? Or would you rather go out on your own and try to find a job, with your limited skills? I don't think you have the physical coordination to make it as a waiter. You might be able to dig ditches or sort mail." I tried to look away, but her eyes held me. "Think about it, Sam. Think hard. Because those are the alternatives. Either you come up with the music, or you get out."

Outside, the huge trucks grunted and belched in B major. Luc started to say something, but she silenced him with her hand. It was very hot in the dark, cramped room, and I could feel sweat trickling down my ribs. Bridget's eyes were level with mine; she would not look away. The plan was preposterous and it would never work, but it was something new and it might turn out to be interesting. "Well . . . all right, I guess I could try it," I said.

"Good," Bridget said crisply, turning away from me at last to reach for a cigarette. "You'd better start right away. The concert's tomorrow, and Humphrey has to wake up with the music in the morning." She checked her watch. "Isn't it time for you to get him over to the theater, Luc?"

They always arranged for Humphrey to have a day or two to practice on a new piano and get used to a concert hall; and it was Luc who supervised and escorted him. Humphrey could play the notes and memorize music when it was drilled into him, but he was hopeless as far as anything practical was concerned. As well-traveled as he was, he had never had time to learn how to handle money or get around unfamiliar cities or deal with strangers and foreign languages. They never let him out on his own. At the moment he was asleep in the next room.

"But *I* never agreed to go along with this," Luc said petulantly. He was obviously miffed that Bridget had chosen me to come up with the music. "We have to be very careful, if we really are going to go ahead with this implausible scheme. We could easily get ourselves into an embarrassing scandal. There are many considerations. We still have problems to solve."

"Yes? Go on," said Bridget, snapping her lighter. "Out with it, Luc. We haven't much time."

He scratched his stubble. "Well, which composer, for instance?"

"Does it really matter very much?" she said impatiently.

"Of course it does. Some would be easier to fake than others."

"Well?" She looked back and forth between us. "Any ideas?"

Luc put his hands behind his back and stuck out his lower lip. He nodded. "Someone rather simple, of course, if you insist on letting Sam attempt it. I think Haydn might be the best."

"Magyar," I said without thinking, just to disagree with him.

"Magyar!" he sputtered. "But that's preposterous. To try to concoct fake Magyar? They'll laugh Humphrey off the stage."

"They already do. And I'm doing Magyar or nothing."

"Are you sure, Sam?" Bridget said, looking a little worried now. "Do you know what you're talking about? Well?"

But I was thinking. Laszlo Magyar, the wizard of the keyboard, the legendary nineteenth century Hungarian with gypsy blood who could play anything. The pianist who was rumored to have made a pact with the devil in order to achieve his superhuman technique. And who occasionally dabbled in composition by taking gypsy tunes and arranging them as splashy shallow salon pieces. Humphrey had played them often in the past, to great acclaim.

"Well, Sam? I asked you a question."

"He's perfect," I said, feeling brilliant. "He didn't compose much. We have his complete piano works in two volumes. People who know anything about piano music are familiar with all of it; they'll recognize a new piece instantly." I looked from Bridget to Luc. They didn't say anything, so I went on. "You know how flashy his stuff is; even if they don't believe it's real, Humphrey will wow them technically. But his music is also simple. It's just a matter of arranging a little tune and then tacking on big chords and fancy cadenzas. Everybody knows it's just a lot of superficial tricks. That's why we *might*

16

get away with faking it. But to try faking somebody really great, like Haydn? Forget it."

"Well, Luc?" said Bridget.

"Sam, go wake up Humphrey," Luc ordered.

"My pleasure," I said, and left. Suddenly I felt marvelous, better than I had in years. Let him whine and complain. I knew I was right, and that Bridget would let me do what I wanted. Now I was beginning to like her little plan very much indeed.

Humphrey was still asleep in the dim adjoining bedroom. He was a soft mountain under the sheet, with a protruding foothill of a head topped by thick black curls. His blubbery lips opened as he snored. He slept with his hands folded over his chest, his enormous, oddly shaped hands with their broad flat palms and widely spaced fingers that thickened toward the first joint and then tapered curiously toward the nails. I reached over and poked one of them.

Humphrey started, and his little eyes, set close together under one thick eyebrow, snapped open. Large though he was, his first reaction on seeing me hovering over him was to cringe away.

"Time to get up, Humf," I said melodiously. "Time to begin another wonderful day of practicing."

"Uhhh . . ." Humphrey rolled over. "So sleepy . . ."

"I know you're a growing boy, Humf, but ten hours of sleep ought to be enough." I switched on the glaring overhead fixture and pulled open the window shutters, letting in the stifling Italian sunlight, the noise and the fumes.

Humphrey put one plump arm over his eyes. "Uh,

Sammy, it was such a pretty dream," he said hoarsely. "A picnic, on a green field with flowers. And we were next to the water . . . So pretty. You, and me, and somebody else . . . Who was it?"

"No Mama and Papa? You dreamed about getting away from them?"

"No Mama and Papa. Just you and me and somebody . . . else. I can't remember who. But we were all happy. Even you were happy, Sammy. It was nice to see you happy." He took his arm away and gazed up at me with those naive little eyes.

"Very pretty, Humf. But unfortunately Mama and Papa are still with us, and they're not going to be very happy at all until they get you back in your place behind that keyboard." I stepped back to the bed and pulled the covers off. His belly bulged out over the pants of his striped shorty pajamas, and the one button left straining to hold the shirt together was ready to pop off. I poked him on the threadbare thigh. "*Up!*"

He knew enough not to complain or protest. He thumped sadly off the bed and I propelled him from the rear to the bathroom down the hall, then returned to Bridget and Luc.

They were still in their bathrobes. Luc was pouting, but Bridget said quietly, "Go ahead with the music the way you want, Sam. Just be sure to let Luc check it over. He *is* the expert." Luc was probably too dense to notice the sarcasm in her voice. She must have told him that I would be doing the tedious mechanical work and that his job would be to slip in the important professional details. Fine, let the slob think what he wanted. I still felt superior, for the first time in many a year.

Soon Humphrey and Luc were off to the theater, looking like seedy twins in their rumpled, ill-cut black suits, yellowing, open-necked dress shirts, their large hands clutching beaten-up music cases. Bridget departed, chic and preoccupied in a blue linen dress, in search of a compliant doctor and a pharmacy.

I stole one of Bridget's cigarettes and watched myself smoke it in the mirror, trying to look tough in a black T-shirt and American denims. My father's African genes had combined interestingly with Bridget's Irish ones, leaving me with wavy black hair, a tawny complexion, rather full lips and slightly almond-shaped eyes. I basked in the pleasure of bearing no resemblance at all to Humphrey and Luc, until the cigarette began to make me feel sick. I squashed it out, hunted up some music paper, and got to work.

2

"NO, thank you, Mama," Humphrey said as we were about to go out for dinner that evening. "I don't need any pill. I feel fine."

Bridget reached up tenderly to stroke his forehead. "But Humphrey, my lamb, you *look* so pale and wan. This little vitamin pill will only make you feel better."

"But I feel good already," Humphrey insisted, moving toward the door. "Can't we go eat now? I'm starving."

Bridget, Luc and I exchanged a glance. None of us had expected any resistance from the usually docile Humphrey. The plan, in fact, had depended upon Humphrey accepting the pill without even thinking about it. If the pill became an issue, he might remember it the next day. Then, gullible though he was, there was the remote chance that he would put two and two together and not fall for our ghostly explanations. And even if he did, he might mention the pill to someone else, which could mean catastrophe.

Luc and I watched Bridget, who, as always, had the final say. For an uncharacteristic moment, indecision showed on her face as she stood there, poised, the gleaming red capsule in her outstretched palm. Of course she could very easily force him to take it, by accusing him of not practicing hard enough, not playing well, then getting Luc and me to back her up. But was it worth the risk of his remembering it? And was there another more devious way of getting the dope into his system? I could see her weighing and balancing, as we waited silently in the steamy little room.

Then Humphrey turned back from the door. "Is something wrong?" he said, wide-eyed. "I thought we were going to go eat. I'm so hungry I can hardly stand it."

Bridget smiled gently at him and slipped the pill back into the pocket of her suit. "Of course there's nothing wrong, darling," she said, reaching for Luc's arm. "Shall we go?"

The cramped cafe next door to the grimy hotel lobby was very likely the worst place to eat in all of Venice. But for practical reasons, it was the dining spot of choice for us that evening. We made our way past the hiccupping jukebox and arranged ourselves awkwardly at a tiny round table. When Humphrey settled his weight on the flimsy metal chair, it creaked in F-sharp major.

Since the perfume of fishy grease was all-pervasive anyway, Luc, Bridget and I ordered *frittura mista* and white wine. Humphrey asked for three cheeseburgers and, as usual, a Coke.

When the waiter returned with the drinks, our eyes zeroed in on Humphrey's glass as though we had never seen the stuff before. But before Bridget had a chance to make her move, Humphrey snatched the glass and drained it in one gulp. "Nice and sweet," he said approvingly, licked his lips and belched.

"*Ragazzo*," shrilled Bridget. "*Per favore, una altra Coca Cola.*"

"For me?" said Humphrey, when the waiter pushed the second glass toward him. "Gee, thanks, Mama." He reached for it.

"Oh, Humphrey." Bridget's delicate hand shot out and pinned Humphrey's massive one to the stained plastic tablecloth. "Wait a minute. It's not good for you to drink it so fast."

"But I'm so thirsty, Mama. *Please.*"

The veins stood out on Bridget's hand as she held Humphrey's in place; her furious eyes shot out a command at me and Luc. But Luc, shredding his paper napkin, his eyes darting around at the other diners, did nothing.

"Humphrey!" I said, pointing at the street outside the store-front window. "Look out there. I just saw the funniest person go past."

"Huh?" Humphrey said without interest, his eyes on the Coke.

"Oh, he's gone now," I said sounding disappointed. "Come on, Humf, let's go out and look."

"I don't want to," said Humphrey, who would have spent his entire life without moving if he could have gotten away with it. "I'm thirsty."

"Oh, come on, Humf, he was so funny," I said, reaching behind Humphrey's chair. His chronic inertia had inspired me over the years to develop many effective little prodding techniques. With a squeal, Humphrey was on his feet.

"Go on, Humphrey, dear," Bridget said. "Sammy's

only trying to be nice. Your Coke will still be here when you get back."

Sighing, Humphrey followed me outside. Of course I had seen nothing, but I had to keep him out there long enough for Bridget to dissolve the Seconal in his Coke. I looked around quickly, but the usual colorful denizens of the area had unaccountably vanished. There were only a couple of totally ordinary looking people in the distance.

"There," I said, pointing at a little old man in black about a block away from us on the other side of the street. "Did you ever see that old man with the long hair before?" It was feeble, but it would have to do.

Humphrey squinted in the direction of my finger. "No, I don't think so," he said.

I looked back into the restaurant. Bridget was nodding at me. "But he looks so familiar," I said. "I thought you would remember where we saw him. That's why I wanted to show you."

Humphrey shrugged apologetically. "I'm sorry, Sammy, but I just *can't*. I wish I could help you." He shook his head piteously, as disturbed as if he had failed to remember his own name.

"That's okay, Humf. Let's go back inside."

"Have some Coke, dear," Bridget said when we sat down.

"Oh, sure," Humphrey said. He picked up the glass and sipped daintily at it, then put it down, almost full.

The waiter came back to drop off our food. The mixed fry was a pile of limp unidentifiable objects, luke-warm, though at some point they had been fried enough to blacken the batter. The three of us made little headway. Humphrey, however, plunged into his burgers with enthusiasm—and soon after that, drained his Coke. Bridget relaxed visibly, leaning back in her chair for the first time since she had sat down. A little prematurely, it turned out.

After Humphrey consumed some pastries that looked about ten years old, and Bridget and Luc had dawdled rigidly over espresso, we were ready to go. The check had been paid, it was about half an hour since Humphrey had finished the doped Coke—giving him another fifteen minutes or so of consciousness.

Then an English woman wandered in and recognized him.

"Why I believe you're that American boy who plays the piano, aren't you," she said, stopping beside our table. She was clutching the hand of a pale little girl of about ten in a big floppy hat. "You remember, don't you, Sally? We saw him at the Albert Hall last year." She adjusted her glasses and looked Humphrey over again. "Or, at least, I thought there was some resemblance . . ."

"Oh, yes, Humphrey performed at the Albert Hall last January," Bridget said brightly. She believed in public relations, and she was not going to let a fan slip through her fingers. "And he's performing tomorrow night, here in Venice."

"How lovely," the woman said, sitting down heavily at the table beside ours. "Sally plays the piano too, you know, and she just loves it. I can hardly tear her away, isn't that right, Sally? Her teacher is Enrico Slogan; you've heard of him, of course. He thinks she's very talented. He told me that . . ."

Bridget listened politely, trying to appear interested, and looking frequently at her watch. Luc was now meticulously at work on my greasy paper napkin. And I had my eye on Humphrey, who was beginning to exhibit a quirky little smile. Every once in a while Bridget would rise, trying gracefully to get us out of there, but the woman paid no attention.

". . . develops not only the artistic sense, but also a healthy respect for discipline, wouldn't you say? But of course play is very important as well. Sally adores country walks and needlepoint and—"

"What I love is mud," Humphrey interrupted, smiling at the little girl."

"I don't believe I caught that," the woman said, laughing.

"Mud, slime," said Humphrey, his eyes blissful. "I always dream of taking off all my clothes and just wallowing in it. Don't you?"

Now Sally was alert. "Oh, yes," she said in her perfect English accent. "I adore slime."

"Sally!"

"We must go now," Bridget said, standing up and pulling at Luc's upper arm. "Humphrey's had a tiring day."

Now we were all on our feet except Humphrey and Sally. "I love the way it squishes thick and warm between your toes," Sally said.

"It must be wonderful," Humphrey said dreamily. "I never really did it, I just always wanted to. Mama, can we find some mud tonight?"

"Luc and Sammy, will you help Humphrey, please?"

said Bridget. She turned to the woman. "So nice to have met you. Please come to Humphrey's concert. *Teatro La Fenice.*"

"I'm afraid we're leaving Venice tomorrow," the woman said coldly.

" 'Bye, Sally," said Humphrey, standing now, weaving slightly.

Luc and I each took one of his arms and began maneuvering him between the tables. But he was bigger and heavier than either of us and listing unsteadily. "*Scusi.* So sorry. *Scusi.* Oh, I'm terribly sorry," Luc kept murmuring, as Humphrey bumped into people. Fortunately it was not a high class place, and the clientele appeared to be used to young men who had had too much wine. The only really sticky moment came when we reached a grandfather in an undershirt whose stomach prevented him from moving any closer to his table. We managed with difficulty to squeeze past him. But then Humphrey scooped up a huge handful of *Linguine con Vongole* from the man's plate, dragged the dripping strands across the man's bald head and slurped them up before we could stop him. The man's veins bulged; but Luc dropped one or two lira on the table, and we got out of there fast.

Humphrey lurched around the tiny elevator, laughing to himself, and I wondered if the creaking little contraption was going to make it. Once inside our bedroom, Humphrey sank down onto the floor and didn't want to move. "Mud, just give me some mud to explore," he sang tunelessly. I had to slap and pinch him like crazy to get him up into the chair at the little desk. He folded his arms on the desk top and rested his head on them. His eyes slid shut.

Only to open feebly a moment later. "Sammy," he mumbled. "Sammy, I remember now, I remember where we saw that old man. It was . . . he was . . ." His eyes closed again, and at last he began to snore.

In the other room, Bridget was smoking furiously.

"Well, at least Humphrey's not a *mean* drunk," I said.

"Don't be flip, Sam. Is he asleep? At the desk?"

"He's very neatly arranged, and I don't think he'll be moving for another ten hours."

"Well that's a relief," she said, sinking down into a chair. "I suppose we're lucky. That very easily could have been a disaster."

"Well, I *can* think of better places to knock him out than the middle of a crowded restaurant," I said.

"Oh, shut up," said Bridget.

"I think . . . if we do this to him again, we have to plan it differently," said Luc, who still looked pale from the ordeal and was dabbing at his face with a handkerchief.

"The important thing at the moment is the music," Bridget said. "You're sure it's ready, Sam?"

It was ready all right. I had slaved over it for eight solid hours that day. The easiest part had been coming up with the tune to base the piece on: I picked an old American blues song, "Yeller Gal," which I did not think the European critics would recognize. It hadn't been too tricky to write the opening chromatic scale passage, descending to a five of two chord in C sharp, and then a gigantic dominant seventh with some drippy suspensions. Then I went blank. So I leafed through the Magyar book and decided to introduce the theme delicately, with grace notes, the way he does in his fifth rhapsody. The problem was, "Yeller Gal" turned out to have an incredibly banal and repetitive harmonic structure, basically one-five-five-one, repeated to the point of nausea. So I did it with grace notes, then trills, continuing to build, then I modulated up a tri-tone, which sounded pretty weird.

And then I went blank again. But the piece was still less than a minute long, too short even for an encore. I couldn't think of anything to do, and the sounds of the trucks outside were driving me crazy, until I had the brilliant idea of using some truck sounds. So I threw in this big honking diesel blast in B flat and took that around the circle of fifths for a while and then went back to "Yeller Gal" again, this time with tremendous crashing chords at double the original tempo, pouring on the arpeggios. Then I had a sudden stroke of genius and went back through the piece, tossing in some twentieth century jazz blue notes here and there—basically just to see if Luc, or any of the critics, would be astute enough to notice them. When I went over the whole thing at the end, it seemed sloppily tacked together and terribly unmusical, like a patchwork quilt made by a blind seamstress. But by then I was thoroughly sick of "Yeller Gal" and was not about to go over the piece one more time. It was going to have to do; and if Luc didn't like it, he could write a new one himself, for all I cared.

Now Bridget said, "Well, can we see it, please,

Sam? I want Luc's opinion. He may want you to make some changes."

"If he wants any changes he can make them himself," I said, and went back in the other room and got the music out of its hiding place at the bottom of my suitcase. Humphrey was dead to the world on the desk, even though all the lights were on.

I handed the music to Luc without a word, then sat down on the bed and watched him look it over. He scratched his stubble and lifted his eyebrows and hummed to himself, trying to look profound. "Well, uh, not too bad, actually. It just might actually pass," he said reluctantly, after looking at it for several minutes. "Except . . ." He thumbed through it again, trying to find something to correct. "Except right here." He put his fat finger down on the page. "This B flat should be a natural. I insist on it, in fact."

I hopped up to look over his shoulder. It wasn't even one of the blue notes; the dope hadn't noticed them. "Sure," I said casually. "You can change that B flat to a natural. You're the expert."

Luc reached into his pocket for a pen. "No," said Bridget. "Let Sam do it, so the writing will be consistent."

I made Luc's stupid correction, getting rid of the B flat. Magyar's last composition had been Opus 26, so at the top of the first page I had scribbled "Opus 27, no. 1," and then a vague approximation of Magyar's signature. It didn't have to be too close, since it was supposed to have been written out by Humphrey anyway. Now Bridget looked it over, sucking in her cheeks. "Well, it certainly looks sloppy enough to be authentic," she said, "just in case anyone wants to see it. And you both say it's going to sound all right. So the only question is, can Humphrey learn it in one day?"

"Sure," I said. "It's just a lot of cheap tricks. It's right up Humphrey's alley."

Before she went to bed, Bridget spread the pages out on the desk beside Humphrey and wrapped the fingers of his right hand around the pen I had used.

Humphrey had always been gullible and submissive. But recently he had begun to show a few faint glimmers of independence, as witnessed by his stubbornness earlier that evening. I wondered, as I slipped into bed, if he was going to be as much of a pushover as we expected.

HUMPHREY was still asleep when I woke up in the morning, the music in place. He had drooled over the closest sheet. I opened the shutters and stomped noisily around the room, and he began to mutter and roll his head. Bridget heard me and came to the door in her bathrobe, already smoking. "Now you're sure you've got the story straight, Sam?" she whispered.

"After all the times we went over it last night, I think I know it better than my own name," I said.

"Shhh! He's coming to," said Bridget.

"Mmmmf," said Humphrey, and rolled right off the chair onto the floor—a rude awakening for him, and the person downstairs as well. Luc appeared, and he and I rushed over to prop Humphrey back in place. For a moment Humphrey sagged down on the desk again; then he blinked and looked up at us. "Hey," he said thickly, rubbing his bleary eyes. "My head feels funny. My pillow fell . . . huh?" He sat up slowly. "I can't . . . hey, I'm not in bed."

"Well, you did tell us not to disturb you, dear," Bridget said, all motherly concern.

"I . . . what?" Humphrey said. He shook his head like a puppy, pushed the hair out of his eyes, and looked down at the music in front of him for the first time. "What's all this?"

"Your precious music that you just *had* to finish last night," I said, glancing at one of the pages. "And it better be good. The lights kept me up half the night."

"Wha . . . what are you talking about?" Humphrey said, looking up at me, groggy and confused. "What's the matter with my head?"

"You mean you don't *remember*?" said Bridget.

"Don't remember *what*?" Humphrey asked piteously.

"The story about the voice in your head, and the music you heard, and making us leave you alone so you could write it down," I said. "The whole crazy routine you went through last night. Are you trying to tell us you don't remember it?"

"Are *you* trying to tell me I wrote this?" cried Humphrey, his voice cracking.

"Humphrey, my little one," soothed Bridget, elbowing me out of the way to bend over and stroke his forehead. "Tell me, darling, what *do* you remember?"

"Nothing different," Humphrey began, shrugging. "Just . . . Now wait a minute," he said slowly, closing his eyes and shaking his head again. "Now let me see . . .

We went downstairs to eat, and uh, we saw that funny little old man, right, Sam?" I nodded. "And, uh, then . . . I think there was a lady and a little girl, but that's kind of fuzzy, and . . . and that *is* all I remember. I don't remember anything after that at all!" He sounded frightened now.

"Luc, what do you think this means?" Bridget said melodramatically.

"Let me see this," said Luc, picking up the music and fumbling with it. I went and stood beside him and looked at it curiously myself, as though I had never seen it before. "Let's see now, the pages appear to be numbered," Luc went on. "Page three, page two, page one . . ."

"Hey, look what Humphrey wrote here!" I said, sounding shocked. "Opus 27, Number One, by *Laszlo Magyar.*"

The three of us stared at one another for a moment. Then we all turned to gaze in silence at Humphrey.

He looked miserable. "But . . . but I don't get it," he moaned. "Why can't I remember? What did I do?"

Bridget was holding his hand now. "At dinner, you began acting a little strange, rather distant," she said quietly. "When we came upstairs, you said you had a headache. Then you began complaining about noises from the next room, someone talking in a foreign language and playing music. But none of us heard anything, and I began to be worried. I wanted you to go right to bed, but you refused. You shouted at me to leave you alone." Bridget looked away from him sadly, getting the most out of her big scene.

"I *shouted* at you?" said Humphrey, aghast.

"You sure did," I said, with one of my nasty chuckles. "I could hardly believe it was you, Humf."

"Perhaps it wasn't Humphrey," Luc said portentously.

But Humphrey didn't notice. "Then what happened? Tell me, please," he begged, squeezing Bridget's hand.

"Well, then you started making these strange, guttural sounds. No one understood you, but it did sound rather slavic. I wanted to call a doctor right away, but your father said to wait and see how you were this morning. The last thing you said in English was to demand music paper and a pen. Then you started writing away, and you absolutely *refused* to stop and go to bed. So finally we just gave up and left you alone, there was nothing else we could do. And this morning, there you were, asleep at the desk, with the music you had written. I must say, darling, I don't understand it at all."

"Come on, Humphrey, tell us the truth," I said. "The whole thing was an act, right? You're just pretending you don't remember."

"But I *am* telling the truth. I don't remember anything. None of it." He looked up at Luc, pleadingly. "Is that really what happened, Papa? Did I really write that music?"

"Yes . . . you did, Humphrey," Luc said, looking down uncomfortably at the carpet.

Humphrey reached out. "Can I see it for a minute?"

Luc handed him the music, and Humphrey looked over it carefully, page by page, shaking his head. "I still can't believe it," he said. "I don't know how to write music. Why can't I remember it?"

"Are you *sure* you don't remember anything?" I said, trying to sound suspicious.

"I told you I don't," Humphrey insisted. "Why would I lie to you, anyway?"

This was my cue. Ideally, of course, the idea of Magyar's ghost dictating music to him should have come from Humphrey. But I, for one, did not believe Humphrey was imaginative enough to think it up himself. And we all agreed that, no matter how much we prompted him, we could not seriously count on Humphrey to come up with the idea on his own. Which meant that it had to be fed to him. But it was also of the utmost importance that the three of us remain skeptical, at least at the beginning. Humphrey knew we didn't believe in ghosts and even he would see through us if we pretended to believe right away. So the only way to remain skeptical but at the same time plant the idea in his head was to do it in the form of an accusation—from mean old Sam, of course.

"Why would you lie?" I asked him. "Oh, come off it, Humphrey, we're not that gullible. I mean look at this." I gestured at the music in his hand. "That whole act you put on last night, and now this music with Magyar's name on it. You might as well just come out and tell us that his ghost came and dictated the music to you. Obviously that's what you're trying to make us believe, isn't it?"

"No!" Now he sounded offended. "Mama, Papa, is that what you think? That I'm trying to play a trick on you?"

"Well . . ." Bridget said, squeezing his hand and looking away.

"But I'm not, I promise I'm not!" cried Humphrey, more upset than ever. "You have to believe me! I'm telling the truth. I don't remember anything. Oh, why did this have to happen?" He rose up out of the chair and threw himself down on the bed and began to sob.

This was the crucial moment. We had fed him the idea. If he didn't latch onto it now and start trying to convince us, then there wasn't much else we could do without becoming terribly obvious. We waited, listening to him cry. Then Bridget sat down beside him and began patting him on the back. Luc and I stood beside the desk, not looking at each other.

Eventually his sobs hiccupped to a stop. His breathing gradually became normal. Finally he turned over on his back, one arm thrown across his forehead, and said in a small voice, "Do you really think it might be possible?"

"What might be possible, dear?" Bridget said vaguely.

"That . . . that the ghost of Magyar came and dictated that music to me," Humphrey said, and I knew we had passed the first hurdle.

Now we could begin worrying about Humphrey's concert that night.

3

IT MUST have been a rotten summer for concertgoers in Venice. Or perhaps there was a sudden influx of ignorant but culture-starved tourists. Whatever the reason, Humphrey had a better house that night than we had any right to expect. When I looked back from my place in the front row at curtain time, I saw far more occupied seats than empty ones. Recently it had been the other way around.

Humphrey was very eager to perform his new piece, of course.

Once he had begun to believe that the music might have come from his own hand with some sort of supernatural help, he was immediately burning to find out what it sounded like. He was not musical enough to tell just from looking at it, though; he had to try it out on a piano. So Luc and Bridget trundled him off to the theater, where he was scheduled to practice that morning. I went along too, just for kicks.

It had probably been an elegant theater once, a not-too-large, horseshoe-shaped hall with elaborately carved boxes. But it had seen better days. Pigeon droppings had eaten away at the facade, giving it a leprous appearance. Inside, the cupids and muses on the ceiling had cracked and faded, leaving many of them without faces or hands; the red plush seats were gashed in places, the carpet threadbare.

There could be no complaint about the piano, however, a marvelous old Hamburg B-type Steinway. Humphrey rubbed his hands together hungrily as he approached it. Luc and I leaned over him as he spread out the music on the rack and set his fingers on the keys.

He's a terrible sight-reader. It took him nearly an hour to get through the piece once. I began to be seriously worried that he would not be able to learn it in time. Luc kept giving me nasty looks behind Humphrey's back; he probably thought I had made it especially difficult on purpose, just to show Humphrey up. Now why would I do a thing like that?

I didn't dare look at Bridget, who watched from the dimly lit house. After the first half-hour she could no longer sit still and began pacing the aisle and chain smoking. We all knew that Humphrey had to do the piece that night. It was his last concert. And since he hadn't played Venice for a year, we were pretty sure that some name musicians would show up—the kind of people who, whether they fell for our scheme or not, would be most likely to rile up publicity. But because of Humphrey's dying reputation, this was the last time we could hope such people would bother to come. It was now or never.

It was agony, listening to Humphrey stumble ever so slowly and painfully over the notes. It must have been frustrating too for Bridget and Luc not to be able to berate me for doing a bad job; they had to keep their mouths shut in front of Humphrey, of course. But fortunately Humphrey, feeling an author's pride in what he believed to be at least partly his own composition, was determined to learn the piece of trash. The second time through it took him only half an hour; the third time, fifteen minutes. By the sixth time it almost began to resemble music. After four hours, Humphrey was rattling the thing off with his usual dull and expressionless aplomb.

Bridget came up onto the stage as he finished. "Well, that sounds a bit better, Humphrey," she said. "But do you still insist on playing it tonight?"

"Oh, please, Mama. I learned it good, didn't I?"

"You know you'll be questioned about it," she said, sighing. "What do you think, Luc?" Her acting was getting better; she really sounded as though she didn't approve.

"Well . . . maybe we should humor the boy," said Luc. "He has worked hard on it. But only as an encore, *if* you earn one," he admonished, shaking his finger at Humphrey.

"I will, I will," burbled Humphrey, bouncing up and down on the piano bench, which squeaked in C sharp minor. "I'll play better than I ever did before."

"Then you'd better do some work on your other pieces," said Luc, looking at his watch. "We only have a few hours until they have to tune the piano."

"But then how can I memorize this?" Humphrey asked.

How, indeed? This was a problem even I hadn't

thought of. Of course Humphrey played everything by memory. It helped to create the illusion that he was a real musician, though it was an onerous chore. It took Humphrey endless hours to learn anything by heart. I remember nearly going berserk when he was working on Chopin's opus 25, no. 2, the F minor Etude. It's incredibly repetitive, and the rhythmic structure never varies once throughout the whole piece. But good old Humphrey had to grind it out over and over again, four hours a day for two weeks, before he got it through his thick head. I still feel nauseated whenever I hear it. Certainly there was no chance that he would be able to memorize my little ditty, which was about the same length but a good deal less predictable. Not that they could blame me. Bridget would have had to think of the scheme weeks ago if she expected Humphrey to memorize anything. We were lucky he was capable of learning the notes in one day.

"But what are we going to do?" said Luc, not even attempting to hide the sudden quaver in his voice. "He can't just carry these scribblings out onto the stage. That's unprofessional."

"Now just wait a minute," Bridget snapped at him. We watched her as she clenched her teeth and brooded. Then she smiled quickly at Humphrey. "Actually, it might not be a bad idea if he did use the manuscript. It might lend a certain authenticity to the . . . ridiculous claim he's going to make about the music's origin. Yes, I think it might even be better this way."

So Humphrey was going to bring the music out on stage—*if* he got an encore.

IT WAS two minutes past eight, and I was waiting impatiently for Humphrey to waddle out to the piano when I became aware of a genteel uproar behind me. I turned around to look. Everyone else was looking too. Of all people, the famous pianist, Pitzvah Prendelberg, was making his way down the aisle, a gorgeous blonde leaning on his arm. She looked vaguely familiar. I could hardly believe it when they reached the first row and sat down in the seats next to me. This was fantastic luck, better than anything Bridget had imagined. Prendelberg was a top international virtuoso, as well as a notorious playboy. Any pronouncement he might make would find its way not only into the music pages, but into the slick gossip magazines as well. Now it was up to Humphrey to do his stuff.

There was a shocked tittering when Humphrey finally did make his appearance; many of these people had probably been expecting a little boy. "We can only hope his playing has matured also," Prendelberg murmured snidely to his companion, in English. Perhaps she was an American.

Even after ten years, Humphrey still looked sheepish and uncomfortable when he stepped out before an audience. He blushed faintly, his lips were pressed tightly together, his eyes downcast. He sat down, breathing heavily, and waited for a moment. Then he wiped his profusely sweating hands on his pants—no matter how Luc tried, he could not rid him of this embarrassing habit—and launched into the Bach *Italian* Concerto.

The first movement could have been worse. He remembered to put in a couple of pianissimos and even a mild crescendo—though for the most part he cranked the music out at his usual unvarying heavy forte. And though he left the dynamics entirely out of the third movement, the notes rippled out flawlessly at an incredible pace, approaching a metronome marking of 160 to the half-note. It sounded as ridiculous as a record played too fast, but it was still impressive in a mechanical way. The second movement, however, made the audience squirm. It's supposed to be slow and velvety and serene, the whole point being to render the jumps in the left hand smoothly, without using the pedal. Humphrey obediently kept his foot on the floor, but the phrasing was beyond him. The notes came thumping out one by one, separate and rude, relentless. It couldn't have sounded less musical if it had been played by those Swiss bell ringers who have to run across the stage between notes. It was so miserably bad that even after the machinelike but brilliant third movement, the applause was feeble indeed. Prendelberg made a nasty face and didn't even bother to clap.

On to the Schubert A Major Sonata, opus 120. Again, an almost impossibly fast rendition of the last movement, following a grossly unfeeling and muddy performance of the second. (So annoying of those classical composers to keep throwing in those sensitive second movements!) And on to Ravel's *Jeux D'Eau*, technically perfect but utterly meaningless, without any delicacy or liquid feeling. Prendelberg actually groaned aloud when Humphrey banged out the first notes. I began worrying that he wouldn't even stay until the end.

Wisely, there was no intermission. We had learned the hard way not to give the audience a chance to escape before the concert was over. And the program was short. Humphrey finished with Stravinsky's *Trois Movements de Petrouchka*. It had certainly been a triumph on Luc's part to train Humphrey to negotiate all those changing meters. And it was the most successful number on the program, being mostly loud and fast anyway.

Nevertheless, the applause at the end was embarrassingly weak. Humphrey bowed stiffly once, then ran off the stage. Before he even hit the wings the applause had diminished to a few single bursts. Already Prendelberg, shaking his head in disgust, had risen to his feet and was starting to move away.

But after about one second in the wings Humphrey lurched back onto the stage, propelled from behind by invisible Bridget, clutching an untidy bundle of music paper in his hand. "For my encore . . ." he began.

A dismal sigh went up from the audience, many of whom were already scurrying out the back doors. Prendelberg kept moving, determined to leave. But his companion, taking pity on Humphrey, or perhaps just feeling uncomfortable about so conspicuously walking out, tugged at Prendelberg's arm. He sank unwillingly back into his seat, swearing quietly and looking at his watch.

"Uh, for my encore," Humphrey croaked, "uh, I will play a piece by Laszlo Magyar, uh, Impromptu, opus twenty-seven, number one."

There was a confused rustling and whispering, and a few bursts of rude laughter. "The fool can't even get his opus numbers right," Prendelberg said, not too softly.

"What do you mean?" said the blonde woman. She had a New York accent.

"There's no such piece. The last thing Magyar wrote was Opus twenty-six, number three. God knows what the imbecile's going to play now. I just hope it isn't one of the long ones."

Tenderly, Humphrey arranged my papers on the music rack. Now Prendelberg seemed reluctantly interested. "Odd that he's using a score," he said, leaning forward. "Wonder where the hell he got hold of it. It almost looks hand-written."

I was nervous now. All of a sudden I felt as though I had to pee and throw-up and faint, all at once. I didn't really care about the piece of garbage, but it was still my first composition, about to be performed in public. Nobody knew who I was, but I still felt naked and exposed. I hoped Humphrey wasn't going to make the music sound more trivial than it already was.

He raced through the chromatic scale passage and banged out the big opening chords with his usual blunt enthusiasm, fortissimo all the way. But then he held the last note of the introduction just a little longer than it was written, as though there were a fermata over it; it sounded right that way. When the theme began, the notes came tinkling out delicately, light and very soft. I could hardly believe it. Humphrey was actually putting some expression into the music.

He kept it graceful and *leggiero* for some time, building only slightly, so that when the first dissonant diesel blast came blaring out, it was a very effective dramatic surprise. Even I, who had composed the piece, wasn't prepared for it. Prendelberg almost jumped out of his seat. The rest of the audience was listening hard.

Prendelberg continued to look more and more puzzled as the piece went on, getting faster and louder. The notes that came pouring out of Humphrey's hands were close to real music now. I sat there listening to it and judging it and had to admit grudgingly that it wasn't all that bad. Even the twentieth century jazz notes, which I had expected to stand out like sore thumbs, instead gave the music a subtle eerie timeless quality.

The piece continued to build and then, unpredictably, suddenly, went quiet and delicate again at the end. Humphrey executed a gorgeous decrescendo, each note softer than the one before. By the last note, exquisitely faint but still definitely audible, everyone was leaning forward.

Humphrey took his hands off the keys and rested them in his lap, not moving from the piano bench. For a long moment there was complete silence. Had they loved it or hated it?

Then a confused babble broke out, which quickly turned into excited applause. It wasn't thunderous, it was not a standing ovation. But when Humphrey finally got up and stood there blushing and bowing a couple of times, the waves flowing up at him from the audience were almost as enthusiastic as they had been when he was a darling little prodigy.

I was baffled. I couldn't imagine what had gotten into Humphrey. That afternoon, his playing of the piece had been as dull and unmusical as ever. Tonight he sounded good. Where did he get that touch of real artistry?

Humphrey left the stage, was pushed out to take

another bow, and then retreated again to the wings. The applause slowly died; they were enthusiastic, but not enough to demand a second encore. Beside me, Prendelberg was on his feet. "I just wonder where the hell that non-existent music came from," he said.

"What do you mean, 'non-existent'?" said the New York blonde.

"I mean Magyar never wrote that music. I don't know who did write it or where he dug it up, and I'm just a little bit curious to find out what's going on."

He took her arm and ran up the three short steps onto the stage. I went up right behind them. Several other intense-looking people were also going up on stage and back to the dressing room, to confront Humphrey no doubt. It was going to be an interesting little session. I hoped Bridget's performance would be as intelligent as Humphrey's had been.

The door to the dreary little cubicle where Humphrey changed into his tuxedo was already open. Within stood Humphrey, rumpled and perspiring under the single bare light bulb that hung from the ceiling, flanked tensely on either side by Bridget and Luc. Behind them you could see a plank table along one wall, a small cracked mirror and Humphrey's street clothes strewn squalidly on a folding chair.

It was a tight squeeze, once Prendelberg, still with the blonde, three scholarly-looking men and a stern-faced woman had all pushed into the tiny space. I hovered just outside the door, peering around their large bodies to watch the action. None of them knew that I even existed, which was just as well, I suppose.

45

There was a brief flurry while they shook Humphrey's hand politely, uttering meaningless remarks in accented English. "Uh, very interesting performance." "Quite a technique, young man." "You certainly beat merry hell out of that Steinway, my boy." But they quickly ran out of things to say, because no one could honestly congratulate him on his performance. In the awkward silence, Humphrey wiped his hands on his tuxedo jacket. Bridget, filling the room with smoke, fought to keep her grim smile in place.

Finally Prendelberg said, "Curious piece, that encore."

"Indeed," said one of the men. The stern woman sniffed.

"Not one I'm familiar with," Prendelberg went on craftily. "And not really a typical Magyar composition, either."

In the background though I was, when Bridget heard that she zeroed in on me instantly with one of her blackest looks. I slid out of range behind Prendelberg's large rear end.

"But it makes rather a stunning ending to a recital," he continued. "Odd, that no one else has ever performed it. Would you mind telling me who published it?"

Humphrey began cracking his knuckles, which sounded like cap pistol shots in the bare cubicle. He didn't say anything, waiting for Bridget and Luc, who usually did all the talking. But this time they were not going to come to his rescue—the less they said, the more convincing it would be. Surprised, Humphrey turned to Luc, who only looked down at the floor. With panic in his eyes, he swung around to Bridget. "Don't crack your knuckles, Humphrey," she said.

"Peters is definitive edition of Magyar, yes?" the stern woman said solemnly, in a Russian accent. "But this thing you play, is not included, no?"

"Er, I . . . uh," observed Humphrey, shifting his weight from one foot to the other, his blush deepening. He began cracking his knuckles again.

Bridget lightly touched his hands. "We told you what would happen, Humphrey dear, but you insisted on playing it anyway," she said. "Don't you feel you owe your audience an explanation?"

"It's . . . it's not published," Humphrey blurted out. "It's new. Nobody knows about it yet."

"I see," Prendelberg said, nodding. "A new composition by a man who died in 1903, well over fifty years ago. I'm afraid I still don't understand."

"I can't help it," said Humphrey, his voice rising to a miserable squeak. "I'm sorry. I didn't want it to happen. It just came to me."

"It *came* to you?" said one of the men. "But then you composed it, my dear boy, and not Magyar."

"But I don't know how to write music. I never did it before," Humphrey explained, his head trembling slightly, his eyes wide and alarmed. "I don't even *remember* doing it. I started hearing funny noises, and a voice, and then I . . . that's the last thing I remember. Then, in the morning, I . . . there was the music." His eyes were filling up with very genuine tears. "Don't be mad," he pleaded, looking at Bridget.

It was beautiful. No one could have sounded more

sincere and heartrending than Humphrey did. He had even obligingly "remembered" hearing a voice and music, which of course had only been our suggestion the morning after. I was impressed; Bridget really knew her stuff. Now, stroking his hand and biting her lip, she managed to appear concerned, but also a trifle embarrassed.

"So!" Prendelberg lifted his chin imperiously. "You are claiming that Magyar, in spirit form, used this boy as a medium to compose a new work, yes?"

"*Please!*" Bridget said with a laugh, cleanly detaching herself from any such ridiculous notion. "I'm afraid we made a little mistake, that's all."

"We never should have let him play it," mumbled Luc, who was watching Prendelberg with an expression of doglike adulation.

"Of course we shouldn't have," said Bridget. "And I do apologize for the confusion. It's just that the poor boy *yearned* so to perform the thing. And he does work so hard."

"But he did write the piece himself?" Prendelberg pressed her. "That much you do know?"

"I'm afraid he did," Bridget said with a casual shrug. "He just got into an ugly mood, which isn't like him, and then insisted on staying up half the night and scribbling it down. Now he says he doesn't remember. Of course we're worried about him. It's some sort of medical problem I'm sure. It's of no concern to anyone else, really. And since Humphrey is very tired, I think it might be best if you could all leave us alone now."

She had guts all right. Magyar's ghost had only just

been brought up, and already she was asking them to get out.

And Prendelberg was ready to go, tightening his grip on the blonde. "I would suggest," he said, "that if he ever has one of these episodes again, you'd be wise to keep the results off the concert stage. Come, Tina."

This was the only opportunity we would have to put over this crazy hoax on the music world. And was this going to be the end of it, this empty little fizzle? After all the work I had done?

"Wait. Give me moment, please," said the Russian woman, stepping toward Humphrey. She was not solemn now; her eyes were fixed on Humphrey with intensity, and blotches of color had appeared on her bony cheeks. "Is manuscript? May I examine, please?"

"Oh, well, I suppose so, if it won't take too long," said Bridget. "Where did you drop it anyway, Humphrey?" she asked him indifferently.

"I have it here," Luc said. He fumbled around with a music case and brought out the sheets. He held them out to the woman, and I could see his fingers tightening on the papers. I didn't blame him for wanting to pull them away from her. She sounded like an expert. Who knew what flaws she might find that could give the whole thing away? If only I had worked harder at making it authentic!

She looked the pages over carefully, her tongue poking out between her thin lips. The others watched over her shoulder. "Is not Magyar's handwriting, of course," she murmured.

"Well, it's not mine either," Humphrey said defensively, protective of his precious music. It gave me a funny feeling to see how proud he was of my composition.

"Yes. That could be," she said. She turned to address the others. "See how many changes, how messy, how composer is unsure of ideas." She pointed with a long finger. "See how he makes impatient blots with ink where he doesn't like, how ugly he writes, how feeble and shaky the stems of notes, how disorganized is working habit. Signs of confused, neurotic mind."

Bridget actually had the gall to flash me a wicked little smirk, even at that tense moment.

"My God," said Prendelberg. "Don't tell me you're taking this nonsense seriously!"

At that point I became aware of footsteps and heavy breathing behind me, but naturally I was too preoccupied by what was happening in the dressing room to turn around and see who it was.

"I do not say I believe." She gestured at Humphrey. "But boy is natural, anyone can see. Though music is odd, yes. . . . Of course, music is clearly twentieth century, not nineteenth."

My heart sank. I closed my eyes to shield myself from whatever lethal glance Bridget might be aiming at me now.

"Music is not Magyar we know," the woman went on implacably. "But *is* foolish and trivial and empty, structure is weak and immature, is nonsensical harmonic progression, is insult to civilized mind." She was shaking the papers at Prendelberg now. "In short—emotion is exactly right! Is what Magyar would write in twentieth century."

My knees went weak with relief. Now I looked at Bridget. Her face was drained of color, but she managed to cock an eyebrow at me.

"And you, Pitzvah," this marvelous Russian woman was saying, "You, of course, know nothing of recent experiments in Soviet Union, of research on psychic phenomena, very scientific, very controlled. This is not only case I observe. You want to know if I take seriously? Yes, I take seriously, very seriously. Why not?"

"You mean you believe in his ghost?" cried Prendelberg's blonde, clasping her hands together and making an excited little hop. "Oh, I'm so glad! I always wanted to believe in a ghost."

There was a babble of Italian behind me. I felt a rude push, and before I knew it, two *paparazzi* had squirmed into the dressing room and were madly snapping pictures of Prendelberg and the girl, who was apparently a celebrity in her own right.

"Oh, no, no, don't take pictures of me, I'm a mess!" she cried, giggling and grinning at them as she spoke. "Humphrey is the one you should be photographing," she explained, switching to broken Italian. "Did you know, a famous composer's ghost comes and makes him write music. And the experts *believe* it!"

After that, it was a while before we got out of the theater. When we finally did leave, we were too excited and exhausted to pay any attention to the shabby little old man who was waiting patiently in the unlit alley outside the stage door. Humphrey scrawled his autograph on the man's program without even glancing at him. It was too dark to see what he looked like, though the old guy did seem to be opening and closing his mouth as if he had something to say. But we brushed right on past him before he had a chance to get it out.

He did manage to croak feebly after us as we hurried down the narrow cobblestone street, something in garbled English that might have sounded like, "Mixmaster of the mind . . . sold you a B natural . . ."

At the time, I hardly gave it a second thought.

4

WE SPENT the morning after the concert, as always, reading the local papers in the hotel room. On this day, the reviews were unusual.

Actually, Humphrey only listened. Even learning to read English had been a terrific struggle for him. And though he had had more exposure than most to other cultures, his entire non-English vocabulary consisted of "hello" and "thank you" in two or perhaps three foreign languages. His non-verbal nature made things convenient for us, because we could easily skip over the main body of the foreign reviews without his being aware of it.

I wasn't really fluent in Italian, though I knew enough words to get the gist of things. Since Humphrey's self-confidence had to be maintained, I denied myself the pleasure of translating aloud to him such passages as:

> Throughout the concert, which seemed to go on eternally, politeness only prevented us from holding our hands over our ears, or from flinging soft, rotten objects at the stage. Why such rage, you may wonder? Who is being hurt

by this obtuse creature who plays the piano worse than a pig? I will name the victim: Music itself. Only a deaf man could fail to be offended to the deepest bowels by such wanton desecration . . .

And so on. Much like the reviews we had become used to in recent months—though these did have an exuberant Mediterranean piquancy. To shield Humphrey from such opinions had become an automatic response.

Though most of them began by deploring Humphrey's performance, when it came to the encore they changed their tone, however reluctantly:

The anomaly was the encore, a curious piece attributed to Laszlo Magyar, which the young man played with something more than rudimentary musicianship. The fact that he is capable of playing with something approaching warmth and intelligence makes one wonder all the more why he should plow through the music of truly great composers as though it were so much dirt.

Perhaps the answer lies in the peculiar claims made about the composition, supposedly a "new" work by the pianist-composer who died at the turn of the century. The performer actually admits to having written the music himself the night before, in a kind of trance about which he remembers nothing. One could only laugh, were it not for the fact that Alexandra

Nitpikskaya, Professor of Musicology at Moscow University, asserts that the music does possess an uncanny authenticity, well beyond the capabilities of the boy who wrote it.

In our humble opinion, the music did exhibit a fiendish, melancholy, calamitous brilliance that made us sit up and take notice. Where, indeed, did it come from?

"Read that part again," demanded Humphrey, lolling smugly on Bridget's bed. "I like that part."

I kind of liked that part myself. But I would have liked it a lot better if I had received some credit, instead of having to watch Humphrey bask in unearned praise.

"You want to hear it again, Humphrey?" I said. "Okay, I'll read it again. Oh, but look here! I think there's something I accidentally skipped earlier on. Just let me read this first, before I—"

"Sam!" Bridget was carefully putting on makeup, but her reflection in the mirror caught my eye. She had been up earlier than anyone and probably had the reviews memorized. "I don't think you skipped anything, Sam. And I'd like to hear that bit about *Humphrey's* piece again, too." She looked back into the mirror. "I don't know if I myself would call it a 'brilliant' composition. More like serviceable, I'd say. But you have to admit that Humphrey did play it well, and *that* helped to put it over."

The bitch! Coming up with the music was the trickiest part of the plan, our most vulnerable spot. And I had done it; in fact it had worked better than we had hoped. Yet the only praise she had given me was that one cocked eyebrow in the dressing room the night before. Maybe I didn't like her little scheme so much after all.

But before I had a chance to respond, Luc, whom she had sent out to track down more periodicals, burst into the room. "Look!" he said panting, waving one of the sensational Italian tabloids at us. "This isn't even a local paper! We made the second page. And a picture, too!"

"Starlet Applauds Psychic Pianist!" screamed the headline. Underneath was a fuzzy picture of Humphrey in the dressing room holding my music. Beside him, the blonde was leaning forward to study the music, a posture that happened to emphasize her deep décolletage. The two of them, in fact, had so much plump flesh between them that Prendelberg was pushed almost entirely out of the picture, appearing only as a dark blurry line at one edge. Nor was his name mentioned in the caption under the photo, I was glad to see. The article raved on and on about how the starlet believed utterly in Humphrey's communication with "the other side," though it did devote a short paragraph or two to the Russian expert who agreed with her. Prendelberg was referred to in passing as "another pianist," who happened to be the starlet's escort. We were very lucky indeed that she had been there to lend some pizzazz to the occasion. And we were even more fortunate that Madame Nitpikskaya had been present to contribute a much-needed element of authenticity.

Still, it was a shock when the phone rang shortly

after Luc's arrival and we were told that she was down-stairs in the lobby and wanted to come up at once.

Humphrey, who sat up expectantly, was eager to see her. Not so Bridget and Luc. The Russian had already done more for Humphrey's career than we could reasonably have expected. All that was needed from her now was for her to go on believing and leave us alone. A closer examination of Humphrey on the home front would improve nothing and would only give her the opportunity to discover that something fishy was going on. Bridget's first impulse was to get rid of her.

But she couldn't. As our most important ally, they owed her the common courtesy of inviting her up. And to turn her away when she already believed would only arouse suspicion. Bridget really had no choice, I was glad to see. For though I was a little apprehensive myself, I was also very curious to hear what else she might have to say about my composition.

"You go down and bring her up, Luc," ordered Bridget. "And take your time about it." Then she hastily finished her *toilette* while Humphrey and I raced around the room hiding dirty stockings and underclothes and soft-drink bottles and old newspapers and crumpled tissues—Bridget was neat on the outside but a slob underneath. As we heard the elevator clanking toward our floor she said, "I think you'd better keep out of the way, Sam, in the other room. We don't want to confuse the issue."

"Hey, hold on a minute," I protested. "I have just as much a right to hear—"

"Do as I say, Sam," she snapped.

57

"But it's my thing, and I want him to stay," asserted Humphrey, attempting to wield his newly restored importance. (This was the most publicity he had received for over a year.) "Why can't he stay, anyway?"

"Because I say so," said Bridget, in a voice like liquid nitrogen.

"And I don't need any help from you, Humphrey!" I said, and slammed the door as I left the room.

As disappointed as I was, I could understand why Bridget wanted me out of the picture. I don't think she was really worried that I would purposely give anything away out of resentment of Humphrey—it had been years since I kicked that photographer. The real reason was that she wanted to play down the fact that there was another member of the entourage who knew something about music, and who therefore could have written Magyar's composition. And as it turned out, it would have been disastrous indeed if she had allowed me to stay.

Listening at the keyhole, I could hear much of what went on. The preliminaries were quickly dispensed with, and very soon the Russian woman was quizzing Humphrey exhaustively about his experience. Humphrey was as convincingly simple and obliging as he had been the night before. He was also a little freer with the imaginary details. (Did he really believe them, or was he aware that he was making them up?) I would love to have seen the look on Bridget's face when he said, "I kind of felt like I was fighting against a . . . a force or something, that wanted to take me over and use me, and . . . it was using music to get at me, so I just gave in, and after that, I don't remember anything."

I could hear papers being rustled. "You don't really believe there's anything more to this than Humphrey's imagination, do you?" Bridget said.

"Maybe yes, maybe no. Controlled research only way to know. But first . . . I have little test we can do here and now, please."

"Oh, how interesting." Bridget's laugh was as warm as shattering glass. "If only we had more time to—"

"Will take only moment. I have pen and paper here. If you will please each write name."

There was an uncomfortable silence, finally broken by Humphrey, who said, "Sure, why not?"

"Surely, you don't imagine either of us could have . . . forged this," Bridget said, sounding shocked and a bit insulted.

"I imagine nothing. Is unscientific. I only believe data."

Of course Bridget could not refuse. Although if I had been in the room, with my own signature very much like Magyar's on the manuscript, I don't know what she would have done. I crouched by the door, once again forced to appreciate her amazing foresight as I listened to the pen scratching.

Then Humphrey said, "What about Sam?"

I winced, and very quietly began inching away. What an idiot Humphrey was! Maybe if I hid in the closet they could tell her I had gone out.

"Sam? Who is this Sam?"

Now the silence was very long, and very unpleasant indeed. At last I heard Luc clear his throat, and Bridget started to say something.

But Humphrey did a very strange thing. He interrupted Bridget. "Sam," he said. "Uh, Sam is . . . our cat."

"Your cat?" said Nitpikskaya. She began to laugh. The others joined in merrily.

I didn't feel like laughing. I was baffled. What was going on in Humphrey's head? Was it possible that he suspected the truth?

"No, is not necessary to find cat," the Russian woman said. "Now let me see here. Yes . . . yes, is as I thought. Signatures completely different. Music composed by another personality altogether."

"But that's just *ridiculous*," Bridget said a little too vehemently. "I'm not sure it's good for Humphrey to give him such ideas. Especially after all that embarrassing, vulgar fuss in the press, which I was hoping we could avoid."

"Please," said Nitpikskaya with authority. "Now I make offer. Please come to Soviet Union, to clinic in Moscow. Is center for study of psychic phenomena. Boy is very special. I beg you to consider."

Bridget gracefully declined, explaining that Humphrey's schedule was too full. In the end, she did allow the Russian to extract a hesitant "maybe," just to get rid of her. Before she left, she again expressed her excitement about my music. It had been a successful interview, all in all. Except that I was confused by Humphrey's lie, and hearing him praised for my work made me angry.

I waited until the elevator was on its way down and then burst into the room. The sight of Humphrey bemused and gloating with self-admiration increased my irritation. "I don't *like* being called a cat!" I snarled.

"Oh, shut up, Sam!" said Bridget. "He was only trying to help."

Humphrey looked at me wordlessly, hurt and bewildered. His expression of wounded innocence was intolerably annoying. "But why did you do it, Humphrey? Why did you lie?"

"I just thought . . . maybe you were busy and wouldn't want to come in and do that silly thing, just because of what happened to me. I didn't want to make you mad, Sammy; that's the only reason I said it. I'm sorry it bothered you. You can have one of my comic books."

"That's thoughtful of you, Humphrey," I said, feeling a bit guilty. "But next time, just keep your mouth shut in the first place, okay?"

The next day the picture of Humphrey and the blonde showed up in a glossy gossip weekly that had one of the largest circulations on the continent. That was fun, and it was very nice that Bridget's little idea had worked so well. But it had still been Humphrey's last concert. Where did we go from here?

Even Bridget didn't know what to do next. We bickered half-heartedly. Only Humphrey remained buoyant, humming sections of "Yeller Gal" to himself and talking about it endlessly. It was a relief when he went to bed.

I was about ready to turn in myself, even though it was only nine-thirty, when the phone rang.

"Yes, what is it?" Bridget said listlessly. Then she brightened. "Yes, certainly . . . Well, *hello*, Geoffrey."

Geoffrey is Humphrey's agent, in London. It had been a while since we had heard from him.

"Yes . . . oh, you did? Good, I hope . . . no! You're kidding!" She raised her eyebrows at Luc. "What do you mean, genuine? I . . . Oh, Geoffrey, don't be silly. Humphrey just had a peculiar little fit, a sort of attack of creativity. I can't help what they . . . Yes . . . Why that's *marvelous*, Geoffrey." She snapped her fingers at Luc, who rushed to fetch a pen for her. She began scribbling on the back page of a magazine. "Go on . . . what was that Milan date? Yes . . . yes, go on . . ."

I caught a glimpse of myself in the mirror, watching her with my mouth hanging open, looking almost as stupid as Luc did. I quickly shut my mouth and picked up my book again, pretending to be indifferent.

"Of course you'll hold out for as much as you possibly can, Geoffrey. This will support it, believe me. And a percentage too, like we used to get. Yes . . . yes, I'll let you know. Thank you, Geoffrey. V*ery* nice speaking with you."

I put my book down when she hung up. "Well?" Luc and I said in unison.

"Milan, next week," she said. "And after that, Geneva. It's been *years* since we played Geneva!" She lifted her head triumphantly. "What did I tell you? I knew this would happen. We're on the way again. Luc, darling, run and get us some champagne, or whatever they call it here. This is cause for celebration."

But after the initial excitement, she quickly became thoughtful. I caught her eyes returning to me again and again over the rim of her paper cup. She was up to something.

She came out with it soon enough. "I hope you're still full of ideas, Sam," she said.

"Ideas? What ideas?"

"Music, of course. Humphrey needs a new encore, fast. I want him to make a bigger splash in Milan than he did here."

"But I just finished the first one. And it wasn't easy. Can't he use it again?"

"He can't keep trotting out with that same tired old piece. The audiences are going to want something new. It has to be immediate. It has to be a world premiere. That's what gets people excited."

"But what if I don't have any more ideas? What if I can't come up with another piece?"

She watched me as she sipped. "You'll come up with one," she said.

THERE WAS a great deal of confusion as we boarded the train two days later, between dealing with our baggage and fighting with the tourists. Amazingly, we did manage to get a compartment to ourselves, though an odd medicinal smell lingered in the narrow, airless space, and a package had been left behind on the dusty seat.

"Sam, run and see if you can return this to whoever forgot it," Bridget said. It was easy enough for her to be gallant when I was doing the legwork. "Hurry, the train's about to leave."

The package was wrapped in old yellowed newspapers. I picked it up and raced down the corridor to the doorway at the end of the car. The train was already pulling away, but I waved the package at the people on the platform and called out, "Anybody leave this? Anybody want this?"

Heads turned, but no one claimed the package. I unwrapped it slowly as I meandered back through the creaking, swaying corridor. When I saw what it was, I stopped outside the door to the compartment.

Bridget rapped on the glass, and then Luc pulled open the compartment door. "What happened, didn't anybody claim it?" Bridget said. "Sam! What's the matter? What is it, anyway?"

"It's a book," I said. "In English." I felt like throwing the thing out the window.

"Speak up, Sam! What book is it?" she demanded.

"The Secret Life of Laszlo Magyar."

5

"BUT IT'S such a weird coincidence," I said for about the tenth time, as the train rattled through the gritty environs of Venice. "Who left it here? I don't understand it. It's . . . I don't like it."

"It's a lucky coincidence, if you ask me," Bridget said. The train wailed in D minor. She was excited about being on the road again and was not going to let herself be unnerved by a mere book—especially a cheap, shoddy edition like this one, which was obviously worth nothing. "After all," she went on, looking at her nails, "it can't do you any harm to learn a little more about our famous ghost, can it?"

She was right about that. Anything else we claimed to be Magyar's would have to undergo at least as much scrutiny as the last piece had, and I could no longer afford to be so recklessly haphazard about putting the music together. The more I knew about Magyar, the less likely I would be to make some stupid blunder that would give everything away. But it was hard for me to believe that finding the book was only a coincidence. It was too neat. On the other hand, who could have known that we would be sitting in this particular compartment? It was impossible to explain, and it made me uncomfortable. Still, there was nothing to do but read the book, an English translation of a work originally published in Austria.

I was still reading when we reached Milan.

Magyar was illegitimate, naturally, the son of a Hungarian count and a gypsy dancer. Born in 1850, he grew up as a kitchen boy on his father's estate. He was not a favorite of his father's wife, the Countess, nor of his older half-brother, the legitimate heir. Little Laszlo saw his real mother only at infrequent intervals, whenever her tribe happened to show up in the neighborhood, and they had to meet in secret. But she exerted a powerful influence on him.

They couldn't keep him away from the piano. Starting at the age of three, he would sneak into the music room and pound away for hours. At last the Count, who had fond memories of Laszlo's mother, engaged a teacher for him, over the protests of the Countess. The boy progressed rapidly. It was not long before visitors to the estate began spreading tales about the gypsy servant lad, who had an elfin charm and played the piano like an angel.

The Count was pleased by Laszlo's growing reputation. Not so the rest of the family. There was an ugly little incident at hog-butchering time when Laszlo was twelve, but he did manage to get his hand out of the meat grinder before any permanent damage was done— though not without severing his half-brother's left thumb with a larding needle, an act that did not endear him to the Countess. His home life, in fact, grew so disagreeable as his playing continued to improve that at fifteen Laszlo ran away.

The records of the next five years are hazy, as Magyar roamed Central Europe with his mother's tribe, and I skimmed quickly over the chapter. The only specific piece of information was a newspaper account of a Bösendorfer grand vanishing during shipment from Hamburg to Prague, a robbery that was never solved.

In 1868, Magyar's single-thumbed half-brother, who had become an amateur scientist, died mysteriously while collecting botanical specimens in the Carpathians. A large boulder inexplicably dislodged itself from a rocky outcropping and mashed his head to jelly, just as he was bending over to pluck a specimen of *Hyoscyamus Niger*. No one could find Laszlo to tell him the news. He was also unavailable when the Countess met her untimely end in a freak accident a year later. For no apparent reason the docile old mare she was riding suddenly went berserk, catapulting her into the farmyard feeding trough, where she was battered to death by an enraged sow. Not until a year after that, in 1870, did Magyar return to his father's estate.

It was fortunate that he showed up when he did, for shortly after his arrival the old Count began to fail, and it would have been tragic indeed if his only living relative had not been by his side to sweeten his last days with music. In his journal, the old man writes touchingly of his son's spectacular playing, which usually went on all night in the room immediately adjoining his sickbed. "The music almost seems to weave a kind of spell," he observed in one of the later entries, "saturating my spirit with a deep disorienting frenzy, releasing me from the bondage of such trivialities as food, water and sleep, all of which seem abhorrent to me now. Only the music matters. I will brook no more interference from those busybody physicians with their noxious potions, and have sent them all away." He died a week later. Laszlo inherited everything.

Magyar's first public performance in Prague the same year caused an immediate sensation. After that he wandered restlessly, impelled perhaps by his mother's blood, performing in all the great cities and before all the crowned heads. He travelled by gypsy cart, taking his piano with him wherever he went, practicing even as they scaled mountain passes and jolted over rough forest tracks.

As relentless as his quest for technical perfection was his pursuit of romantic liaisons. Many a peasant maiden, catching sight of the wagon with its gaily painted arcane symbols and hearing the passionate music from within, would be compelled to follow along behind. Without stopping the music, Magyar had only to lift his left hand briefly from the keyboard to beckon her inside. Sometimes the girl would be discarded only a few miles down the road. In other cases, she would be kept on for a few weeks and dropped off wherever they happened to be at the moment Magyar became weary of her. Many of the younger ones never found their way home, stumbling instead into unsavory predicaments in the big cities.

Magyar did make several life-long attachments that

transcended these ceaseless casual encounters. He was a frequent visitor at the castle of the Romanian Princess Marie-Therese, often leaving wild revels in the early hours of the morning to retire to her private suite in a tower overlooking a foaming gorge, where he would practice until dawn. There was also the poet Alphonse Thibauld, with whom Magyar haunted certain notorious dens near the wharves of Marseilles and Tangiers. Thibauld rhapsodized about their bizarre passion in several sonnets and an aubade, but his poetry was so cryptic that no one, save the author of this book, ever realized whom he was talking about. And of course there was Mother St. Cyr, the Abbess of a remote convent in the Urals, who would shed her habit and vanish without explanation from her cell whenever Magyar was in the vicinity. It was whispered among the sisters that under Magyar's influence she once led a Black Mass involving human sacrifice at an ancient basalt slab beside an eldritch tumulus on a mountain pass. But it was only a rumor.

Even the worshipful author of the book, who claimed to be a descendant of Magyar, couldn't deny that his idol's lifestyle was not altogether wholesome. Though it had no basis in fact, one can understand the pervasive rumor about the pact with the Devil, which Magyar never tried to dispel, but instead seemed to enjoy. And it was not only his inhumanly dazzling technique that caused people to wonder about Satanic powers. For though he indulged wantonly in every imaginable vice, Magyar never seemed to age. In 1900, when he was fifty, his body was still slender and lithe, his face fresh and unlined, his vigor, and his various appetites as powerful as they had been at twenty. How much longer would his youth have persisted? the author wondered. We will never know, for at the age of fifty-three Magyar tripped in front of a streetcar in a suburb of Düsseldorf. Not only was he neatly decapitated, but both his hands were also cleanly severed at the wrist. His head, according to the book, is still soaking in formaldehyde at that remote convent in the Urals. And his hands, inexplicably, vanished without a trace.

AT THE BACK of the book was an appendix, listing all of Magyar's forty or so compositions, with a brief harmonic analysis of each. It was a little drier than the biographical part of the book, but very convenient for me. Most of the pieces were based on gypsy tunes, and the harmonic progressions, as Nitpikskaya had said, really weren't logical. Whatever effect the pieces had was due for the most part to Magyar's smashing technique. I certainly couldn't have picked a better composer for our project. He was exactly the kind of obnoxious person whose ghost, if you were idiotic enough to believe in such things, would be likely to come back and wreak havoc on the living. Better yet, as a composer he was a superficial slob, and therefore easier than most to copy. As we neared Milan, I was almost beginning to look forward to dashing off another one of his compositions.

It was just as well that my attitude was positive, because we didn't have much time. Usually concert bookings were made far in advance. But the pianist who had been scheduled to appear in Milan had suddenly been taken ill, at the same time that Humphrey's name had appeared in the papers. Since the people in Milan desperately needed someone to fill the empty spot in their series, and since no musician with a serious reputation would play at such short notice, they had asked Humphrey. The concert was in two days. Already it was time to repeat the procedure we had executed so awkwardly in Venice. This time, perhaps, we could manage to avoid some of the mistakes we had made before.

We weren't rolling in wealth yet, and the hotel Humphrey's agent had booked in Milan was just as cramped and dismal as the one in Venice had been. But there was a halfway decent desk in one of the rooms. I began working that very night.

I chose another American folk song for my theme, a tune called "Green Corn," which was almost as simpleminded and repetitive as "Yeller Gal." Still, it had a lot of bounce, and I was inspired by the wildness and total freedom of Magyar's life. He was an independent guy, if nothing else, and so I tried to get an independent feeling into the music. It wasn't too hard. I just blithely scribbled away, ignoring all the rules, tossing in totally unexpected harmonic changes and ghastly conjunctions of chords. This time, instead of jazz notes, I used jazz rhythms. It ended up even more outrageous than "Yeller Gal," but I wasn't worried. Now that I knew what an uncontrollable eccentric Magyar had been, I was confident that no one could *prove* the music to be beyond his imagination. They might not agree about it, but the more controversy the merrier.

When I showed it to Luc the next day, he grunted and toyed with his slimy lips. Finally he said, "I don't like this C sharp major chord. Better get rid of it."

The C sharp major chord happened to be one of my favorite parts. It came right after a G major seventh, and I enjoyed the weirdness of the progression. "Oh, come on, Luc. Let me keep the C sharp major," I said, "It's no stranger than a lot of things Magyar did."

He didn't even have the courtesy to answer me. "Bridget," he said, "I've asked Sam to get rid of this C sharp major, and he's balking."

Bridget looked up from her magazine. "Get rid of the C sharp major, Sam," she said.

"But it's a great chord there," I protested.

"The C sharp major is out, Sam," she said, with finality, and went back to her magazine.

So I acquiesced, carelessly blotting out the C sharp major and replacing it with a far more predictable chord. I had liked the chord, but big deal. Now that I was finished with the piece, I hardly cared about it at all. It was rubbish anyway.

The night before the concert, I was sent out to pick up food and bring it back to the privacy of our rooms. We had learned from the last experience. I bought sausage and bread and cheese and wine and Coke, and four *cannoli* for dessert. In my usual clumsy way, I kept fumbling with the packages as I walked, not really looking where I was going, and so I collided with someone as I was entering the hotel. I dropped the package of *cannoli*, upside down, and I was so busy picking it up that I didn't even get a look at the person I bumped into, who rudely hurried away without a word. All I noticed was a peculiar medicinal smell that was faintly familiar.

Bridget ordered Humphrey to wash his hands, and so this time she had no trouble at all dissolving the pill in his preprandial Coke. We picnicked messily in Bridget and Luc's crowded little room. I sawed off big hunks of salami and cheese with my Swiss pocket knife, and we tore the bread apart with our hands, paying no attention to crumbs. The *cannoli* were a little flattened, but still better than anything we had eaten in Venice. The cuisine here was reputed to be more interesting in general, and I looked forward to tomorrow night, when, if the concert was a success, we were planning to celebrate afterwards at a decent restaurant.

Then Humphrey and I settled down for a quiet evening in our room, I with *Buddenbrooks*, and Humphrey with a pile of horror comics. It didn't matter that they were in Italian, since Humphrey only looked at the pictures anyway.

Humphrey began giggling about forty-five minutes after we had eaten. I did my best to ignore it. But Humphrey's mirth only increased, and after five minutes of it I put down my book and said, "All right, Humphrey, what's so hilarious? Maybe if you tell me about it, you'll shut up."

"Oh, but Sammy, it's so funny, I just can't help it," he said, trying to choke back his laughter. "Here, you look at it." We were lying on twin beds, which they had managed to cram into a room only big enough to be a single. Humphrey rolled over to hand the comic across to me, stretching out his arm to avoid the effort of sitting up. "This page right here."

The drawings were sloppily printed in lurid reds and

greens. A horde of witches, blood dripping from their mouths, were dismembering a helpless male, limb by limb. A figure in a red cloak, presumably the devil, directed them. As I read, Humphrey continued to chortle merrily at the mere thought of it.

"Humphrey, this isn't funny, it's disgusting," I said as I tossed the comic back. I was actually a little unnerved by his ghoulish response. "What is there to laugh at?"

"Oh, it's just . . ." Humphrey shook his head and wiped the tears out of his eyes. "Just . . . they think . . . the other one looks like that." And he was off again.

"Stop it, Humphrey!" I said, sitting up and grabbing his foot and squeezing it hard. "Stop it this minute! You're acting screwy."

"Oh . . . I just," said Humphrey, finally pulling himself together but still grinning sheepishly.

"But it's not one bit funny. What do you mean by 'the other one' anyway?"

"But Sammy, you know as well as I do," he said, sitting up earnestly. Then he swayed and closed his eyes. "Hey, what's the matter?" he said. "How come I feel so dizzy?"

"Humphrey, *what do you mean?*" I persisted, standing up and looking down at him.

"Oh, *you* know," he said, smiling again and rocking back and forth. "Feel so funny all of a sudden. Warm and cozy."

I grabbed his hair and pulled his head back. "Tell me what you mean," I snarled.

I wasn't pulling gently, but he was anesthetized by the pill and just went right on smiling. "Oh, Sammy, don't be silly. You *know* what I mean," he said. "And it's so pretty on the island, out in the sunlight, the water and sky so bright . . . so much space . . ."

I gave up. I wasn't going to get anything sensible out of him. And if I didn't hurry, I wasn't even going to be able to get him out of bed and into position. Grunting, I pulled him to his feet and guided him over to the desk and into the chair. He obligingly slumped forward onto his arms, singing quietly, and in a moment was asleep.

I said nothing that night to Bridget and Luc about Humphrey's odd response to the comic book. I'm not sure why. I just didn't want to talk about it. I did my best not to think about it either. After we arranged the music and the pen under Humphrey's arms, I retreated back into *Buddenbrooks*.

I didn't sleep very well. I dreamed that the four of us were back on the train, squeezed into the tiny compartment with a huge Bösendorfer grand. Humphrey pounded on it furiously, but it produced no sound at all. An audience of witches from the comic book milled around in the corridor and outside the slowly moving train, hungry for our flesh. I knew that if Humphrey stopped playing, the train would stop too, and they would devour us.

When Humphrey awoke the next morning, he was not nearly as bewildered and confused as he had been the time before. The grogginess wore off quickly, and he was more impatient than ever to get over to the theater and learn the new piece for the concert that night. Bridget stayed in the hotel, but I had to go with Humphrey and Luc in case they had trouble reading the notes.

I went reluctantly, already thoroughly sick of "Green Corn." The scheme was beginning to make me anxious. I tried to tell myself it was foolish to brood about what that strange old man had said to me and to worry about Humphrey's peculiar behavior. I was trapped in it, after all, however much I was beginning to dislike the plan. The only sensible thing to do was to try to make the best of it, since it was too late for me to get out of it now.

As before, Humphrey had a rough time learning the notes. But if I had made the harmony more conventional, and therefore easier to learn, or the rhythms less tricky, then the piece wouldn't make the bizarre splash that was necessary to get the audience riled up. I did whisper to Luc, toward the end of the hot, grueling, tense afternoon, that next time, if there was a next time, we would do well to get Humphrey the music a couple of days in advance.

"Well, that's your department, isn't it, Sam," he said with a mean little laugh. He was always a lot bossier when Bridget wasn't around. "It's your own fault you waited until Milan to start this piece. I'd suggest you start preparing another one right away."

"In that case, you can finish teaching it to him," I said. "I'm sick and tired of it." I left the theater and gloomily wandered the streets for several hours.

But as the concert got closer, my mood began to change. It was impossible not to be excited and curious about how the audience was going to respond. There were no seats for us this time, since we had been called on such short notice and the series was already sold out, so we had to watch from backstage.

The theater manager and the concert organizers, who had made it clear that they had strong reservations about Humphrey, finally left for their box seats just before eight o'clock. A fat stagehand in an undershirt remained, occupying the only chair. The four of us stood in the small stage-right wing, squeezed together among curtains and ropes, waiting out the last few minutes.

As usual, Humphrey was overcome by stage fright. He paced, clutching a wad of toilet paper (graciously provided by the management) upon which he continually wiped his dripping hands. He nodded abstractedly at Luc's final bits of advice, while his unhappy eyes darted around as if searching for some last minute reprieve that he knew wouldn't be coming. And I realized for the first time that I was very glad not to be going out there. I even felt a pang of compassion for Humphrey.

Bridget had been checking on the house from the near edge of the curtain. "Okay, Humphrey, the time has come," she said at last. "Good luck, darling." She pecked him on the cheek.

"Already?" lamented Humphrey. "Can't I just wait another—"

"Get out there and play," she said.

Humphrey took a deep breath, clenched his fists and marched out. Luc only just managed to get the toilet paper out of his hands before he hit the stage.

It was a repeat performance of the concert in Venice—the same repertoire, the same technical prowess, the same obscene poverty of musical expression. It had been bad enough watching as an anonymous member of the audience. From backstage the debacle was even more embarrassing. The audience, observed from a distance, seemed less like a harmless, if restive, group of individuals and more like a hostile mob.

When Humphrey came barrelling toward us at the end of the scheduled program, there were actually a few jeers and catcalls over the heavy rush of the audience getting away. Perhaps the concert in Venice had been a fluke. Perhaps this group would laugh "Green Corn" off the stage, and I felt a desperate itch to destroy the manuscript before Humphrey exposed it to them.

But Bridget didn't give him a chance to pause or think. *"Speak clearly!"* she whispered as she thrust the music into his hand and spun him around toward the piano again.

"For my encore, uh, I will play a piece by Laszlo Magyar, uh, Capriccio, opus twenty-seven, number two," recited Humphrey, in the rote Italian we had drilled into him. The audience did not become noticeably quieter. I cursed them silently, suddenly aware of my own hot sweat, and squeezed my eyes shut. It was all I could do not to cover my ears.

After the first chords, the house went silent, just the way the interference vanishes when a clear channel on a radio is found. The notes jangled and bounced out into the theater, restless and exuberant, the barbaric harmonies clanging. It sounded almost funny, and I would have laughed if I hadn't been so tense—not to mention astonished, once again, by Humphrey's performance. He played the disorderly concoction like a musician, with delicacy and bravado and artful intelligence.

That was unnatural enough, and it should have gnawed at me more, but vanity got in the way. The music worked, and I allowed myself to bask in a self-congratulatory feeling of creative power. I even flattered myself that I might have had something to do with Humphrey's shockingly adequate performance. "What the hell got into Humphrey anyway?" I whispered to Luc as the piece drew to its close. "He almost sounds like a musician. I bet my music did it to him."

"Don't be ridiculous," Luc said loftily. "It's obviously because of the way I've been coaching him."

The applause interrupted me in mid-snort. Humphrey came beaming out to meet us, and as he stood breathing heavily in the wing, the applause only grew. This time he needed no prodding at all to go back on stage. As I watched him take bow after bow, ever so humbly and shyly, it suddenly hit me: *that was my applause.*

And where was I while Humphrey was out there piggishly lapping up the reward? Cringing in the wings. And when the critics and fans came swarming backstage, I was still cringing, keeping out of the way, obediently shunning all attention. I was nearly blinded by the sensation of longing and injustice—nearly, but not quite. Bridget's steely eyes penetrated the fog of envy and rage like klieg lights, keeping me chained in my place, a hungry observer at the feast.

This time they were not as skeptical as they had been before. They accepted Humphrey's unaffectedly told story as though they were looking forward to hearing it—which they probably were, having read the earlier articles. And Nitpikskaya was back again, vouching stolidly for Humphrey over Bridget's shrill protestations. She repeated her invitation to the clinic in Moscow, more urgently now because she had to return to the Soviet Union the following day. When Bridget once again declined, she extracted from her the name of Humphrey's agent, so that the director could write with a formal proposal. The reporters ate it up. There was even another photographer snapping pictures. Apparently Humphrey didn't need starlets any more. The snowball was gaining momentum.

I had shared in the general elation following Humphrey's performance in Venice. This time I shared nothing, keenly aware of being the mistreated outsider. And so, not being intoxicated like the others, I was the only one who really noticed the little old man waiting outside the stage door; I was the only one who felt the shock of recognition, the only one who heard what he croaked into Humphrey's preoccupied, uncomprehending ear.

Thus it was fear, not envy, that dulled my appetite in the restaurant later, though I'm sure Bridget and Luc thought otherwise. After months of eating cheap and longing for such a meal, I barely tasted the garlicky *scampi*, the *osso bucco* with its fresh piquant *gremolata*, the creamy rich subtlety of the *rissotto a la Milanaise*. Even the velvety *zabaglione* went down my unfeeling throat like so much lumpy tapioca.

"Very nice, very pretty and nice," the impossible old man had cackled at Humphrey, ruining my dinner. "You do only one . . . listen, how you say? . . . only one mistake . . . You only forget the C sharp major."

6

WE TRAVELED to Geneva in a first-class compartment. It was uncomfortably small, but the appurtenances were polished, the upholstery was pleasant to the touch, in good repair and not dusty in the least. The others watched as the sunny hills shed their soft complacent curves and cold angular mountains reared up in mist and dampness. I stared at the wall and sulked.

I was angry—and scared. During the night I had been awakened several times by bad dreams about the obnoxious old man. Who was he? What did he want from us? How could he possibly have known about the changes Luc had made in the music? Bridget and Luc had barely listened to me the night before when I told them what he had said after the two concerts, dismissing the incidents as trivial, nothing but misinterpretation on my part. Maybe they were right, but I still couldn't stop thinking about it. Music I had written, which we were passing off as the work of a mysterious and long-dead composer, had precipitated two unexplainable occurrences—and they told me it was just my imagination. Naturally I sulked.

But after an hour or so I began to tire of listening to Humphrey gloat over his latest reviews, so I picked up the Magyar book. Between the ages of fifteen and twenty he had roamed Europe with the gypsies, and on my first reading I had glanced only superficially at that particular chapter. Now I went back to study it in more detail.

The author made an attempt to describe the atmosphere of gypsy life and its influence on Magyar. There were deep forests in central Europe then. At night, the campfire would seem a small thing in the vast sighing darkness under the trees. The talk would be merry at first, as the wineskin made its way around the circle of half-lit, saturnine faces. But gradually the bright logs crumbled to hissing coals, and the stars, dimly perceived through the shifting blackness of the leaves, drifted across the sky, and the conversation drifted with them. This was the time for old family histories, for the trading of gypsy wisdoms and for ancient tribal tales.

Young Magyar did not say much, squatting on a pile of filthy rags at the outer edge of the group around the fire; but he listened and remembered. There was the tale of the white doe who sang with the voice of a woman, whose enchanted music promised to lead the unwary traveler to endless wealth. If he did follow—and it was said that no mortal man could resist her call—she would guide him to a treacherous bog and then vanish, leaving him to be swallowed slowly by the bubbling muck. There was the tale of the wise woman's daughter whose dancing was as fierce and delicate as flame. She performed with jangling bracelets and tambourine in the streets of large cities and was thrown a great deal of gold.

She was faithful to her handsome lover and with the gold bought him silk shirts and velvet trousers and jeweled earrings. But one morning she awoke to find him gone, with his fancy clothes and all her gold. When she learned that he had betrayed her for a highborn lady, she returned to her mother, the wise woman. And within a year, the unfaithful lover's teeth softened in his head, his face withered like a prune, his body grew stooped and feeble, and his skin blistered with pustulent sores. He died alone in a sewer among rats.

When it came to the story of the haunted violin, Magyar would forget to brush the spiders and bird droppings from his hair and would lean forward with special interest. This story was always told by one particular toothless crone. She had heard it in her youth from the only surviving member of the family who possessed the violin, a frail and sickly old man who, the storyteller claimed, actually played her a few notes on the legendary instrument. This person's great-great-grandfather Janos had had the violin made to order by the world-renowned violin builder, Sebastiano of Cremona. When Janos had gone early one morning to pick up the instrument, he found Sebastiano sprawled lifeless across his worktable, his body limp as overcooked pasta and curiously shrunken, as though some vital essence had been sucked out of him. His left hand grasped the neck of the violin, his cracked lips were pressed against one of the F holes. Apparently he had died in the act of making love to the thing. Janos pried the instrument out of the corpse's hand, tucked it under his cloak and got away from the workshop as quickly as he could. Since he hadn't yet paid for the violin, Sebastiano's death was uncomfortably convenient for him, and he preferred not to be seen in the vicinity. Perhaps if he had left even one token gold piece in Sebastiano's moist and cheesy palm, the price he was eventually to pay for the violin would not have been so dear. But perhaps it would have made no difference at all.

Not until he reached the safety of his own wagon in the gypsy campground on the outskirts of Cremona did he touch bow to string. An incredible note came forth, rich, warm, hypnotically intense. Hardly thinking, he let his fingers slip mechanically into a common gypsy tune. Normally Janos was only a mediocre violinist, but the music he produced with *this* violin was rapturous, transformed, more profoundly beautiful and significant than any music Janos had ever heard. When he finally brought himself to stop playing, after what seemed to him only a few minutes, half the day had gone by and it was almost evening.

He flung open the doors of his wagon and cried out to the others in the camp to come and listen. Naturally they were curious about the sound of the new instrument and soon a crowd had gathered. As soon as Janos began to play, he was so hypnotized by the thrilling, celestial music that he lost consciousness of everything else.

A large and slimy potato making contact with his right temple knocked him out of his trance. Reluctantly he lifted the bow from the string and looked around him with hurt, bewildered eyes. The camp was in an uproar. His listeners were gnashing their teeth, holding their ears, cursing, groaning, begging him to stop. Women and children were bending over being actively sick. "But what's the matter with everybody?" Janos cried out. "Didn't you hear the music?"

"Music? Is *that* what you call it?" someone replied. "*I* didn't hear any music."

"It was like the sound of wagon wheels that have never been oiled!" cried someone else.

"No, no, it was like wildcats being slowly disemboweled!" insisted another.

"It caused every fiber of my body to vibrate with feverish loathing," moaned a young woman, wiping her mouth. "May I never experience such sounds again."

"Hear me, Janos," announced an elder of the tribe. "If you again torment the air with such poison, may your hands blacken and wilt like fungi and your eardrums burn forever with the pain of flaming coals inside your head."

This was something of a dilemma for Janos. To his own ears the music of the violin was so exquisitely, addictively pleasurable that already it was misery to refrain from playing the instrument. But apparently no one else found the music so enjoyable. Though Janos longed to ignore their ridiculous protest and play as he wished, he could not ignore the elder's curse. To a gypsy, such pronouncements are very serious indeed.

The only solution was for Janos to spend as much time as possible out of earshot of everyone else. Naturally this solitary behavior resulted in his becoming more and more ostracized by the others—an unhappy situation for the gypsy, who is ostracized by the entire world and whose tribe is his only home. Janos soon became frail and sickly like a man addicted to wine who trembles when deprived of his bottle. On Janos's death, the violin passed to his son.

For every generation it was the same. He who possessed the violin would be hopelessly obsessed by its music, while all others found it made only noise, intolerably repellent. Finally came Janos's great-great-grandson—he who told the story to the old crone—who died without an heir. The instrument was not found beside his deathbed, nor was it in fact ever seen or heard again.

"And when he played it for you," Magyar would ask the crone, "what did it sound like?"

"Ah," she would croak, and pause to inhale deeply on her pipe, stroking the bowl with veined, arthritic fingers. "Ah, such a monstrous sound, like nothing I have heard before or since. Even now, after eighty years, the mere thought of it causes my bowel to writhe like a worm on a fishhook."

"Yes, but what did it sound like?" Magyar would press her.

"Once I was privileged to observe the public execution of a witch" said the crone. "Though her neck was so tough that it took the headsman five strokes, she made no sound at all, until her head was finally severed from her body. When that happened, a kind of sour and whistling wail bubbled out of the exposed end of her throat and persisted for a full minute. That is the closest sound I can think of to the music of the haunted violin."

"But *why* was the violin haunted?" Magyar would ask her, when he was still very young. "Was it because Janos did not pay for it, or was there another reason?

And was it the Devil himself who made it haunted, or someone else?"

"Hush!" commanded the crone. "It is not for us to know the answers to such questions. We observe the patterns, and we accept." And the group would move on quickly to other tales.

Magyar did come to believe that the forces of good and evil in the world—of God and the Devil if you like— were equally powerful and equally unpredictable. But unlike the old crone—who insisted that the pattern of one's life was written on the hand in infancy and could not be changed—Magyar was never willing merely to accept. He loved the story of the haunted violin because of its depiction of the power of music. But he was at the same time appalled by the fatal helplessness of the characters, as well as by the unknowable mystery of the curse. The more he thought about it, the more determined he became that he would never be so helpless. He would take control of the power of music and any other powers that might be helpful and with them determine his own fate. And if this particular old crone did not possess the knowledge and the answers that he needed, then he would search out someone who did.

One autumn night, when Magyar had been with the gypsies for about a year, the group found themselves camped in the mountains, not far from an ancient castle with a sinister reputation. Glancing frequently over their shoulders, the elders traded stories of heads of enemies displayed like hunting trophies in the great hall, of elaborate mosaics made of eyeballs and sculptures of polished bone, of ritual feasts where the succulent flesh of human infants was devoured. Magyar was experienced enough to know that such stories become exaggerated over the years. Nevertheless, he was just as startled as any of the others when an intruder suddenly appeared out of the darkness.

The man lurched into the firelight, gasping for breath, one foot dragging painfully behind him, clutching against his stomach a bundle wrapped in rags. "Help me, please," was all he managed to utter before he toppled into a puddle of mutton grease and vegetable peelings and lost consciousness.

Magyar's mother had always been a hospitable woman, as well as more curious than most about the behavior of the *Gaje*, or non-gypsies. She and Laszlo dragged the stranger into the wagon they shared. She took the responsibility for nursing him back to health. The man's leg was badly wounded, but he turned out to be a strikingly handsome young man. He stayed in the wagon with them for over a month.

"The stranger awakened me to many things, and what I learned from him I shall carry with me for as long as my consciousness exists," Magyar wrote about the experience. But to the dismay of his biographer, he never divulged the nature of what he learned, only that it was of profound importance. The only other reference the biographer made to the incident was to mention that the stranger had left the rag-wrapped package as a token of his appreciation. Apparently Magyar always kept it with him. But the biographer, despite a long and obsessive search, could find no indication anywhere of what it was the rags contained. It was shortly after this incident that the piano was mysteriously stolen on its way from Hamburg to Prague, and soon after that Magyar's *Gaje* relatives began having fatal accidents.

The author of the biography made no attempt to analyze these events, leaving all interpretation up to the reader.

The chapter only made me more irritable than I had been before I read it. It was nothing but coincidental rubbish, and Magyar was merely a self-involved, not very talented eccentric with superstitious tendencies. Only a gullible moron could take seriously the implication that he had used some sort of supernatural power, devilish or otherwise, to kill off his relatives, achieve his fame and preserve his youthfulness. Only a retarded fool could imagine that he might be able to use the same power to effect events after his death, (if he had really died at all), or that the old man I had seen had anything to do with Magyar, or had some secret way of finding out about our hoax. A person would have to be even more stupid than Humphrey to waste one minute worrying about that kind of supernatural nonsense. I slammed the book shut and began struggling to pull open the window.

"Do you have to be so fidgety, Sam?" said Bridget. "What are you doing with the window?"

"Trying to open it, naturally."

"Open it? But it's so drafty in here already."

The window refused to budge. "I just want to open it for a second, so I can get rid of this stupid piece of garbage. I'm sick of carrying it around."

"That Magyar book? But you seem so fascinated by it. And you might need it."

"It's just a lot of made-up stuff, and it bores the hell out of me," I said, still struggling with the recalcitrant window.

"But *I* don't want you to throw it out," whined Humphrey. There was a petulance in his voice that I had never noticed before. "*I* might want to read it someday."

As if he were capable of reading anything more erudite than a comic strip! "Don't make me laugh, Humphrey. There's more than ten words on a page," I said. But I shoved the book back into my bag.

GENEVA GLEAMED, white and clean, the air crisp, the lake like brightly polished glass. I felt as filthy and used-up as old bath water. A couple of English-speaking newsmen and a photographer met us at the station. Humphrey was so eager to get to them he almost knocked me down on the way out of the compartment. He babbled happily at them on the platform while I struggled with luggage and porters. At the hotel, it turned out that there had been some mistake with the reservations made by Humphrey's agent, and there was no bed for me. A narrow and flimsy folding cot with a mattress like cardboard was irritably jammed into the small space between the wall and Humphrey's double bed. Not that I expected to sleep much anyway.

After we had settled in, I left Humphrey with some new comic books and went down the hall to Luc and Bridget's room, which was three doors away from ours and therefore out of earshot. "I just don't like what's happening," I told them. "It's making me nervous and giving me a mental block. I'm not sure I can compose any more. It *was* the same weird old guy waiting after both concerts, I know it was. And each time he knew exactly which note Luc made me change."

I looked back and forth between them, waiting for a reaction. Luc, reclining against the headboard, the thick folds of fat around his navel protruding from beneath his shirt, shrugged irritably. "I always told you you spoil him," he said to Bridget. "We give him a free hand, and now he's complaining about the few minor changes I *had* to make. Next I suppose he's going to demand that I have no say about the music at all."

"No, no, you've missed the whole point." I turned to Bridget. "It's not the changes that bother me. It's the fact that somebody else knew about them. And there's no *way* he could find out. It's just impossible. Can't you see why it makes me nervous?"

Bridget looked at me unblinking for a moment, then went back to braiding her hair. "You're making too much of this, Sam," she said, a hairpin in her mouth. "It could hardly be the same person in Venice and Milan; I'm sure you're mistaken about that. And you said yourself his speech was indistinct. You simply interpreted whatever it was he said in your own way, because of the resentment that was in your mind. I didn't expect you to be quite so petty about it."

I swallowed my howls of frustration. "Please listen to me," I said, with all the earnestness I could muster. "It's not resentment. All I'm really asking is that Luc write the next one instead of me. That's all I want. He *is* the professional; he'd probably come up with more convincing music than my stupid stuff."

Of course, I didn't really think that Luc would do a better job. Moreover, composing the music had given me more real satisfaction than anything I had ever done. Yet now all I wanted was to wriggle out of the project. I had the faint hope that an appeal to Luc's vanity might be a means of escape. "I mean it," I went on. "Any time now, those critics might start seeing through my little things. What we need now is a real professional touch."

But Luc didn't seem flattered at all. If anything, he sounded nervous. "Uh, what do you think about that, Bridget?" he said.

"I think Sam's up to something," she said, with a knowing little tilt of her head. "And of course these fine musical distinctions are way over my head. But it seems to me that things have been working out quite well just the way we've been doing it all along."

"Which means you *don't* want me to start writing the first drafts myself," Luc said, with obvious relief. "I definitely agree."

As I should have known, Luc's laziness took precedence even over his vanity. Why should he bother composing the "first draft," as he put it, when I was there to do all the hard work, and all he had to do was arbitrarily lift his little finger when I was through and make a couple of "professional" changes?

". . . refuse to pay any attention to this neurotic self-indulgence and these transparent little stratagems," Bridget was saying. "It's all too boring and bogus for words, and there's no point to it at all. If you pull yourself together and start behaving like an adult human being, all this nerviness will go away and you'll feel much better, I promise you. Not that you have any choice in the matter anyway. We need a new piece and it's time for you to get to work on it. You've had too much time on your hands, that's the whole problem. Once you get involved in working on something again, you'll forget about being jittery, believe me."

"But I just don't want to!" I blurted out stupidly. "I don't want any part of it any more. It's driving me nuts and *ruining* Humphrey!"

"Don't you remember what I told you the first time you balked?" she said quietly, staring at me. "Let me remind you, just in case you have forgotten. You do your fair share, Sam, or you get out. It's as simple as that."

"I . . . oh, just go to hell, both of you!" I shouted, getting in the last word with my usual brilliance, and left them.

The odd thing was that Bridget, in one respect at least, turned out to be right—though I would never admit it to her. As soon as I began working on the next composition, the miserable uneasiness and the warring emotions I felt really did abate. I was immersed in a puzzle of exceptional beauty and intricacy, a puzzle that only I, out of all the people in the world, was able to solve. Once I had embarked, there was no time to be concerned with anything but the captivating problems at hand. Again I chose an American folk tune, a song called "Pick a Bail o' Cotton," and this time I tore it apart and slapped it back together again in a more outrageous parody of Magyar's style than I had had the nerve, or the skill, to attempt before. I no longer cared what Luc or the critics might think about the music, so

94

I allowed myself the pleasure of throwing in jarring, screamingly unpredictable rhythms and harmonies. And since we were earlier this time, and Humphrey would have two full days to learn the piece, I devised some really awkward and mathematically confusing meter changes, chuckling at the thought of how much trouble Luc was going to have trying to beat them into Humphrey's simple brain.

And at night, twisting on my cot, I tried not to think about the old man. He wouldn't show up in Geneva, it couldn't happen, I was only being morbid. With the pillow wrapped around my head in an attempt to dampen Humphrey's sonorous rumblings, I repeated to myself as the hours slunk by that I had nothing to worry about at all . . .

ON THE EVENING that we drugged Humphrey the third time, we ate dinner in the hotel room again, clearly the only sensible procedure. On this occasion I was sent to a decent restaurant and brought back a bulging carton of *choucroute garni* and several bottles of beer and soft drinks. The first thing Humphrey said to me when I walked through the door was, "I want some more Coke, Sam. I hope you brought some."

It had started to rain while I was on my way home. The paper bag had nearly dissolved, and it was only with great difficulty that I had managed to save what I had. I set down the soggy remains of the bundle and shook some of the water out of my hair. "I'm sorry, Humphrey, but the bag got wet, and the Coke fell out and broke. I almost dropped everything else trying to save it. I even went to two more stores trying to get another bottle, but they didn't have any." It was all true; I had gone to a lot of trouble to procure the all-important beverage. Still, it didn't really tear me up inside to tell Humphrey he wasn't going to get any. "But there's some ginger ale and cherry soda. They're nice for a change."

"But I want my Coke; I always have to have my Coke. I *need* it for . . . for my work. Why did you have to go and drop it, Sam?"

"Oh, come on, Humphrey." I picked up a greasy, lipstick-stained hand towel from a pile on the floor and made an attempt to dry myself off a little. "Didn't you have two Cokes at lunch? Anyway, ginger ale goes better with *choucroute garni*."

"That's right, darling," Bridget said soothingly. "And it's good for your digestion, too."

"But I want Coke," insisted Humphrey, scowling at me.

Humphrey had been such a dim little child that the adulation of the outside world had had little effect on his docile, cowlike temperament. But now that he was older and had experienced a barren period, it was only natural that all the recent adulation had caused even as feeble a head as his to swell. And it was equally natural that I should not be particularly generous about forgiving him the foibles of his fame.

"Can it, Humphrey," I said.

"Well, but why shouldn't Sam go back out and get some?" Humphrey whined, still scowling, but now edging toward Bridget for protection. "What else does he do? I'm the one that plays all the concerts. I'm the one that writes down the music. Why shouldn't Sam take care of—"

"That's right, why shouldn't I wait on Humphrey, the genius? I'm only Sam, the no-talent drudge." Though he towered over me, he backed away as I stepped toward him. "That's a flattering, pretty way for *you* to look at the situation, isn't it, Humphrey? I don't suppose it ever occurred to you that you don't know everything, did it? That maybe I could shatter a few—"

"Sam! Humphrey! Stop it!" ordered Bridget in her most arctic tones. (Though in her voice there might have been—and at the thought I felt an incipient thrill of power—a hot tiny bubble of fear.) "You're behaving like infants, both of you. Humphrey, you can do very well without your disgusting Coke for once. And Sam, if you ever even *think* of saying anything at all, uh . . . disturbing to Humphrey's creativity, then, I promise you, the consequences will be more unpleasant than anything you can possibly imagine." She cast me a glare of such menace that she could have been slowly and thoroughly grinding out her cigarette on my tender eyeball instead of in the overflowing, chewing-gum-filled ashtray.

There was barely enough space for the four of us in the room, and we sat uncomfortably close together as we ate. Humphrey sipped resentfully at his doped ginger ale, toying with the delicately spiced, wine-flavored sauerkraut as though it were mere rotten cabbage. I didn't have much appetite myself. Though I tried to remain aloof, I couldn't keep my eyes away from Humphrey. I didn't like what success was doing to him. His previous indifference to acclaim, which I had always regarded as a sign of gross stupidity, now began to seem charmingly naive. He hadn't been such a bad little dolt after all. Angry as I was, for a moment I almost felt worried about him.

"Mama, why is Sam looking at me like that? Make him stop looking at me."

"Don't be ridiculous, Humphrey," I said, reaching for a magazine. "You know I wouldn't look at you while I was eating."

But I still kept my eyes covertly on him. It wasn't only the changes in his ordinary day-to-day behavior that were morbidly fascinating. I was also watching for signs of the drug taking effect and wondering what nutty things it was going to make him say this time. There was a chance that he might even do something bizarre enough to alarm Bridget and Luc, if I could keep all of us together long enough for them to observe it.

But before we had finished eating, Humphrey pushed his plate away with a deep belch and said, "I don't want any more. I want to go back and read my comic books."

"Letting all that good food go to waste?" I said disapprovingly. "That's not like you, Humphrey."

"But I don't like it. It's . . . icky," Humphrey said.

"Yes, but if you go away, then I might get some of yours," I said. The brat he was turning into might well eat something he didn't like just to keep it away from me.

"Leave him alone, Sam," Bridget said. "I don't think we have to worry about Humphrey being undernourished."

"And he needs his rest," Luc put in. "He's been working very hard."

"Oh, I know," I said quickly. "I was just going to say . . . uh, it might be good for him to get his mind off his work for a while."

"It's too crowded here. I'm going back to my room," said Humphrey, getting up.

But I couldn't let him go. I was determined to keep him in the same room with Bridget and Luc until the drug started to affect his behavior. If they saw how gruesome he could be, then they might begin to understand why the situation was worrying me. Just describing how he had laughed at the comic book wasn't enough. They would never take me seriously until they saw him do something equally fiendish with their own eyes.

In the past, I could simply have asked him to stay up with us, and he would have happily obliged, thrilled that I wanted his company. But these days he was too ornery and pigheaded to pay any attention to a request of mine. I had to create a diversion, to come up with something interesting enough to make him want to stay.

"Wait a minute, Humphrey," I said.

"Wait for what?" he said, moving toward the door.

What could we all do that he wouldn't want to miss? "Well, if you just stayed we could . . ." I searched my mind desperately. "We could all . . ." Then it hit me. "I know! We could all play a game. Wouldn't that be fun, Humf?"

"A game?" Humphrey blinked down at me, puzzled but interested. Playing together was a concept that had never occurred to anyone in our family. "What kind of game?" Humphrey said.

Of course it couldn't be anything with complicated

rules, like cards, or that required imagination, like charades, because in either case Humphrey would be lost immediately. It had to be simpleminded but intriguing. "Well, uh . . ." I almost said "Ghost," but quickly reconsidered. Not only did that particular word bother me somehow, but the game also required a modicum of spelling ability, once again eliminating Humphrey. Was there any game at all that he could play? "Um . . . I know, twenty questions," I said at last. "That's loads of fun."

"Now what's he trying to put over?" Luc asked Bridget. "Does he actually expect you and me to participate in this infantile nonsense?"

"I just thought Humphrey might get a kick out of it. He hardly ever gets a chance to have fun, like other kids. Do you, Humphrey?"

Bridget frowned at me, but Humphrey had been hooked. "How do you play?" he demanded, sitting down again.

"One person thinks of something. An object, a person, anything at all. The others try to figure out what it is by asking questions. They get twenty questions, and they can only have 'yes' or 'no' as the answer. If they guess what it is, they win. If they don't, the one who thought of something wins."

"That sounds pretty silly to me," Bridget said. "Humphrey, you don't really want to waste your—"

"I thought of something, I thought of something!" crowed Humphrey, clapping his hands. "You'll never never guess what it is. Come on, ask me a question. Ask me!"

The object Humphrey was so sure we would never think of was "piano." Though I tried to be as dense as possible, we got it in six questions. But rather than being discouraged by his defeat, Humphrey was eager to keep the game going until it was his turn again.

Luc came up with a metronome, which we got in ten questions. Bridget's choice was the Star of India diamond, which required sixteen. And I thought of a breaded veal cutlet, Holstein, served with a fried egg and anchovies, which nobody got at all, and Luc insisted was unfair.

By now, Humphrey was getting that self-absorbed, giggly look. "It's my turn, and I already thought of one," he said, interrupting Luc in the middle of a petty argument about the rules. (He just couldn't tolerate not having guessed my word.) "I've got one, and you'll never guess it. Come on, guess!"

We established that it was animal, smaller than a breadbox but bigger than a mouse. I immediately thought of food. "Is it something people eat?" I asked.

The question struck Humphrey as peculiarly funny. "Something to eat?" He laughed, rolling back his head. "Oh, I can just see you munching on it, Sammy! I wonder how you'd like the taste."

"Just answer the question, Humphrey," I said.

"No, no." He sighed. "Nobody eats it . . . I mean them."

"What do you mean, 'them'?" Luc demanded. "Are you thinking of one thing or two?"

"Is that supposed to be a question?" said Humphrey astutely. "Because if it is, it has to be yes or no."

"But I don't think it's fair to think of two things," Luc protested. "Guessing one is difficult enough."

"Stop worrying about that and play," I said. "I'll ask the question. Are you thinking of two things, Humphrey?"

"Yes."

"Then what you're thinking of is a little animal and its mate, isn't it, Humphrey dear?" Bridget asked.

"No," said Humphrey complacently. "That makes ten questions."

"Come, Humphrey, it must be," she said. "It's two cute little hamsters, isn't it?"

"No," said Humphrey. "That makes eleven."

"You're wasting questions," I said. "Now, Humphrey, these two animals, are they—"

"I never said it was two animals," Humphrey chuckled, bursting with glee at how he had all of us fooled.

"But you said it was animal and there were two of them," said Luc. "So it has to be two animals, doesn't it?"

"No, it doesn't," Humphrey said, grinning smugly. "That makes twelve questions."

"We'll never get it if you two keep wasting questions," I said. "Let's see . . . two things of animal origin but not two animals. Okay, Humphrey, are they alive or dead?"

"Has to be a yes or no question," trilled Humphrey, in an especially irritating singsong voice.

"Okay, okay. Are they alive?"

"No, they are not alive," Humphrey said.

"But they're not food?" I murmured, then added quickly, "That's not a question, Humphrey."

"Are they something that might be used around the home?" Bridget asked.

This question sent Humphrey into more paroxysms of amusement. "Around the home?" he managed to gasp. "Around *whose* home, I wonder?"

"Just tell me yes or no," said Bridget, beginning to sound annoyed.

"No, no, not around the home," he said.

Two dead things of animal origin . . . Something unpleasant hovered at the edge of my consciousness, but I couldn't get a firm hold on it. No one else was doing any better. In the end we had to give up, completely stumped. "Okay, Humphrey, you win," I said at last. "Just tell us what it is."

Once again Humphrey was helplessly besieged by laughter. It was only after a full minute of struggling, tears streaming down his face, that he managed to choke out the words, "Two dried up, uh, wr-wr-wr—" And he was off again.

"What is it?" I cried, reaching for him. "Out with it, Humphrey!"

"Two dried up human hands wrapped in old rags," he shrieked, and rolled away from me onto his back, beating his hands and feet against the floor and howling with merriment.

7

HUMPHREY made a bigger splash in Geneva than he had in Venice or Milan. The SRO audience demanded three encores, and so Humphrey played all three Magyar pieces. Uncomfortable as I was, resentful as I was, I still had room to feel pleased with myself at the impact the pieces made, played all together like that. Their total unpredictability of mood, their eerie indifference to musical common sense created a sensation of utter detachment from human emotions and concerns, as though the driving force behind them was somehow alien to mankind. They really did sound like music from beyond the grave. The lingering dead silence after each piece only made the wild applause that followed seem all the more out of control. Flashbulbs snapped and flowers fell at Humphrey's feet as he took his final bows. I looked the other way, tensely scanning the audience for a glimpse of the little old man.

Even after this stunning success, neither Bridget nor Luc had anything complimentary to say to me. For the last three days, in fact, we had barely spoken to each other. We had reached an impasse.

Our last real conversation had occurred the night we had drugged Humphrey. At the unexpected conclusion of our game of twenty questions, Bridget, turning away abruptly from the prostrate hysterical Humphrey, had decreed that it was time for him to go to bed. With a significant glance at her, I prodded him to his feet and then dragged him, stumbling and giggling to himself, down the hall to our room. He docilely allowed me to arrange him at the desk, where he slumped forward peacefully.

But I wasn't ready to let him go to sleep. "Humphrey! Humphrey, listen to me!" I growled into his ear.

"Mmmfff . . ." he said comfortably, his eyes closed.

"Humphrey!" I spat at him, and pulled his head roughly back by the hair.

"Yeah? What is it?" he murmured, slowly opening his eyes.

"Humphrey, where did you get that idea about the two hands wrapped in rags?" I demanded. "What made you think of that?"

"The two . . . oh! The two dead hands!" He began laughing again.

But I was no longer in the mood for games. I slapped him across the face. "Pull yourself together, Humphrey! It's not funny. Just tell me where you got the idea."

"But Sammy, don't you know?"

"Just tell me!"

"From The Other One. Who else?" he said reasonably.

"*Who is The Other One?*" I bellowed, shaking him by the shoulders.

He swayed in my hands like a rag doll. "*You* know, Sammy," he whimpered. "On the island, like my dream. I tol' you . . ."

"*Who is The Other One?*"

There was a sharp rapping on the wall from the next room.

"Don' worry, Sammy," he mumbled, barely moving his lips. "He's our friend on the island, you and me, he's our . . ." He slumped forward again, suddenly snoring.

After a couple of further attempts to rouse him quietly, I gave up. But I wasn't finished for the evening. I dug the Magyar book out of my suitcase and marched back down the hall. From outside their room I could hear Bridget and Luc talking in hushed voices, but I was too riled up to eavesdrop. I banged on the door. "It's Sam," I said. "Lemme in."

There was a long moment of silence and then Bridget's voice came irritably from just inside. "It's late, Sam. Can't it wait until—"

"It's not about me, it's about Humphrey," I said, and banged again.

She opened the door a crack. "Sam, this is not the—"

I pushed past her and stalked into the room. Luc, naked and jellylike, was just heaving himself ponderously into bed. I averted my eyes, and before either of them had a chance to speak I demanded, "Well? What did you think of that little performance?"

Bridget pushed the door closed. "I suppose by that you mean Humphrey's behavior tonight?"

"You know that's what I mean. Don't tell me you didn't notice it. Something's wrong with Humphrey;

you know it's not like him to act that way. And he did the same thing the last time you doped him. He was laughing hysterically at this sadistic comic book."

"And . . . ?" she said maddeningly.

"But it's not normal. There's something funny about him. You've got to admit that."

"Sure, I'll admit it." She shrugged. "But he was drugged, Sam, that's all it is. So it makes him a little bit drunk? That's part of the effect, it's perfectly ordinary. Naturally he's going to act a little peculiar."

"Does it say on the medicine bottle that it makes people morbid and ghoulish?" I asked her. "And even if it did, there's more to it than that. There's this book." I held it up.

"What about it?" she said, trying to sound casual.

"Two things," I said, and took a deep breath. "First there's the bundle wrapped in rags that Magyar carried with him everywhere throughout his life. Just like the bundle Humphrey thought of tonight. Except that no one ever found out what was inside it; no one but Magyar ever knew. Got that? And second, when he died his hands and his head were cut off. And they have his head somewhere, but no one ever found his hands. They just disappeared. And because he was such a famous pianist, it was a big mystery for a while. But it was never solved." I stopped for a moment, to let it sink in. They were both staring at me, their faces rigid and alert. "And now," I went on slowly, "sweet little Humphrey, out of the blue, comes up with this tremendously *humorous* concept of two dried-up human hands wrapped in rags. Interesting, isn't it?"

"But surely you must have said something to him about all that," Bridget countered. "And so it was already on his mind, that's all."

"Except that I never did. I never breathed a word to him about what was in this book. I told him nothing."

"Well then, he just must have read it himself," Luc put in grumpily from the bed.

I opened the book and flipped the pages at him. "See all this small print? Hundreds of pages of small print. And you're trying to tell me that Humphrey read this?" I asked him. "You know as well as I do that he has trouble getting through a comic book. And even if he *was* capable of reading it, I know for a fact that he never did. When would he have had the chance? The only time he's ever alone is when he's asleep. One of us is always with him. If he'd ever picked it up, we would have known it. Not to mention the fact that the book has always been with me, either in my hand or in my suitcase. Humphrey has never so much as touched it."

In the silence a toilet gurgled distantly, and somewhere below us a metal door clanged shut and the elevator began its groaning B flat minor ascent. Luc was pulling at his lower lip, his baffled, confused little eyes staring past me at nothing. Even Bridget was at a loss. She started to speak, but her voice dried up in her throat. For the first time I noticed a slight tic just below her left nostril.

Were they taking me seriously at last? "Now do you get it?" I said, beginning to feel relieved. "Can't you *see* why this whole thing makes me nervous?"

That broke the spell. As Bridget moved to the

dresser to get a cigarette, I could see her short-lived doubt and indecision dissolve away; her eyes regained their clarity and focus, her lips went taut and her chin lifted. "Coincidence," she announced, blowing out a thick column of smoke.

"No!" I cried out. "It's too neat for that. It can't be coincidence."

"Then what is it, Sam?" She lifted her eyebrows and smiled nastily at me. "If it isn't coincidence, then tell me what the hell *you* think is going on."

"Well . . . uh, the little old man knowing about the changes in the music, and Humphrey knowing what's in the book and being so morbid. Two scary, impossible things; and we're . . . using this crazy, dead person's name to fool people and make money, it's . . ."

"It's what, Sam? Just give me your explanation."

"But I can't," I said, nearly in tears. "That's what scares me. There's no explanation. We're doing something wrong, and it makes these . . . these impossible, scary things . . ." My voice faltered. "And you can see what a spoiled monster Humphrey's turning into. *He'd* be better off too if we just . . . stopped for a while."

"Oh, Sam, I know it must be difficult for you," Bridget said, her voice softening unexpectedly. She moved toward me and rested her hand on the back of my neck. "It must be frustrating not getting any attention for the music you're composing, I know that. But you must realize that no one would even come to hear it if they knew *you* were the composer and not Magyar's ghost." She squeezed my neck. "It's tough, Sammy. I know the situation isn't ideal. But it's not easy for any of us. All the traveling around, all the hard work we *all* put into Humphrey's performances."

"Then why don't we just go home," I said, feeling like a broken record. "We proved we could pull it off; we showed Humphrey could attract audiences again. We've been lucky so far: no one's exposed us yet. Let's quit now, while we're ahead."

"But that wouldn't be fair to Humphrey—or to you, Sammy." She moved away from me, pacing as she spoke. "You don't know what it feels like to have children, Sammy, exceptional, talented children, like you and Humphrey. It's a kind of privilege—and a *responsibility*." She turned to face me, squeezing her hands together almost in an attitude of prayer. "It would be wrong to deny Humphrey this opportunity to practice his art, to deny him his rightful recognition. And isn't it wonderful to know that you have talent too, Sammy? So what if we have to twist the facts a little? That's still *your* music all those people are responding to. It would be *wrong* to stop it now, *wrong* to hide such talent from the world. Can't you see that?"

She wasn't acting. She really believed what she was telling me. She didn't see herself as pushing Humphrey. She had never seen it that way. Sure, she wanted the money. Sure, she lapped up the acclaim. But she also believed, with all the fierceness in her, that she was performing an almost sacred duty. She wasn't exploiting her beloved Humphrey, she was *nurturing* his talent, in the only way that meant anything to her. It was as though she were giving him a marvelous gift—a gift that I was trying to take from him.

I should have known better than to argue with her about what she believed—she had based her life on it, after all. But, rashly, I plunged ahead. "But I really don't think it's good for him," I said. "He's changing, can't you see that? He's turning nasty . . . The way he was laughing about those dead hands . . ."

"So you expect us to cancel this lucrative season, this *rebirth* of Humphrey's career, because of some little coincidental events that you can't even explain?" she demanded, her voice suddenly harsh again.

"But it's not like that, it's more than—"

She held up her hand, silencing me. "I don't want to hear any more. I have had my last word on this ridiculous subject. Did you set up the music under his hands?"

"No, but—"

"Then what are you waiting for? This subject is finished, permanently. And this conversation is over. Leave us alone now, please."

I can't analyze her power; I can't explain what made her so convincing. All I know is that at that moment I felt like an utter fool. All my worries seemed babyish and trivial. It was humiliating. The last place in the world I wanted to be was their bedroom. Without another word I departed. And I had barely said another word to them since.

NOW, as Humphrey's enraptured audience reluctantly began to leave, I made my way backstage. Not that I really wanted to be there. I had heard my music and would have liked nothing better than to go off and be alone, instead of lacerating myself with the spectacle of

Humphrey surrounded by adoring fans. Yet I couldn't keep away. Though on the one hand I dreaded the little old man, I still couldn't resist being there at the stage door with Humphrey, just in case the creature should appear again. This time Luc had made no change in my composition. If the old guy did show up, what might he say? I had to know. I also had to be around in case the opportunity arose to point him out to the others. If they saw him too, they might begin taking me seriously.

Humphrey's dressing room was packed with reporters, taking pictures, asking him questions in French-accented English, lavishing him with praise for the music *I* had composed, telling him he was a genius. I couldn't bear listening to it. I retreated out of earshot and waited miserably at the far end of the hallway. When I went back about twenty minutes later, I had calmed down a bit. Humphrey, Bridget and Luc were standing outside the dressing room, and there was only one fan left, a tall dark man in a tuxedo, who was deep in conversation with Luc. Naturally they didn't introduce me to him. As I approached, they all turned away without greeting me and started toward the stage door.

"Who is that guy?" I asked Bridget numbly, trotting behind them down the dim cement corridor.

"I can't pronounce his name. He's a big wheel in Vienna. He's arranging for us to go there." Triumph glittered in her eyes. "He says he can guarantee we'll have full houses there for at least a week."

"Vienna," I mumbled, aware of a curious foreboding.

"And he insisted on taking us out to dinner tonight," Bridget went on, sounding girlish. "To one of the most expensive . . ." Then her smile hardened. "Uh, I think it might be best, Sam, if you kept out of the way this evening."

"You mean you don't want me to come?"

"That's precisely what I mean."

"But . . . but that isn't fair. I'm hungry. And I'm a part of this family, too."

In the past, Humphrey would have stood up for me, he would have argued with Bridget on my behalf. Tonight Humphrey said, "He only invited the three of us."

"I'm sure you'll find something to eat near the hotel," Bridget said quickly. We had reached the stage door. "Just smile and work your way through them as fast as possible, Humphrey," she went on, and we pushed open the heavy metal door and stepped outside.

I didn't see the old man at first. I searched the excited group that swarmed around Humphrey, but there was no familiar wizened face. In a moment I was separated from Humphrey and Bridget by a thick wall of people. Then I felt something brush against my arm.

I spun around. The face was shadowy in the dim glow of the bulb over the door, but I recognized the long matted white hair, the sea of deep wrinkles, the thin beak of a nose, the gaps in his teeth as he grinned up at me. "Yeh, yeh, the hands," he chuckled.

"*What?*" I said, feeling sick.

"The hands . . . I, how you say? . . . Is hands. He has the hands."

I started after the others. "Bridget, come back!" I shouted. "He's here, he . . ."

But they were already half a block away, and there

were too many people between us. It was useless. Another wave of faintness and nausea hit me, but I gritted my teeth and turned around again, to force myself to take a good look at the old man's hands, which I had never bothered to notice before, to see if he had any hands at all . . .

But there was no one there.

8

IT WAS autumn in Vienna. Rows of stolid buildings sulked under a sodden sky. Rotten leaves smeared the sidewalks, and the dark river lapped and eddied sullenly beneath windy embankments and slimy stone bridges. The atmosphere might have been a refreshing antidote to the sterile whiteness of Geneva, if only I hadn't been too much of a wreck to notice.

The others, basking in success, did not let my mood interfere with their own ebullience. I was mostly mute, and they seemed to have little trouble ignoring me—though once or twice I was aware of Humphrey's eyes lingering on me with an unfamiliar appraising expression. I didn't pay much attention. I was doing my best not to pay attention to any of them.

The agent had found us another terrible hotel. Formerly an elegant place, it had been refurbished in dreary institutional style, perhaps by the Russians who had so recently left. Once large rooms were divided by flimsy partitions; they sported warped linoleum floors, a heating system that hissed and rattled dementedly, and peevish medieval plumbing, more often than not too dispirited to flush with adequate conviction. The others joked good-humoredly about our accommodations, struggling to outdo one another in pluck and spunkiness. I couldn't have cared less about any of it.

We had almost a week before the start of Humphrey's engagement. A rehearsal studio had been rented near the hotel, and there Humphrey and Luc went to work at resurrecting and polishing sufficient repertoire to fill up the seven scheduled concerts. I, needless to say, was expected to crank out an abundance of new Magyar pieces—enough to keep the audience too excited to notice the way Humphrey played everything else.

I was too demoralized to rebel, though I didn't really expect to be capable of producing anything. But once I sat down to work in our claustrophobically small room, I was surprised to find myself utterly engrossed. I scribbled for long hours, spurred on by the audible bodily functions that came resounding with crystal clarity from the adjoining chambers. Nothing could have inspired me more. I struggled to translate their piquant timbres and mellow sonorities into the language of music. I aspired to break new ground, to create a keyboard technique so expressive that an audience would recognize these familiar sounds immediately. And after only three days, I solemnly presented Bridget with two charming preludes, their tone colors as liquid as the juiciest upper respiratory infection, as well as a lengthy alimentary *divertissement,* in which waves of reverse peristalsis gushed and splattered above a rumbling obbligato of the most profound intestinal motility.

I had escaped so thoroughly into my work that I had succeeded in ignoring the others completely. But on the evening that I finished these three pieces, I began to look around again. And the first thing I noticed, when Humphrey and Luc returned from the studio at around eight P.M., was the shocking change in Humphrey's behavior.

It shouldn't have bothered me, because I was more resentful of him now than ever. And yet . . . somehow I was reminded of the emotion I had experienced in Geneva when I had noticed what the hoax was doing to him. The unearned adulation, coupled now with a brutal rehearsal schedule, were turning Humphrey into a petty, demanding, resentful brat. That amazing simplicity, the open-heartedness that had caused him over and over again to defend even me, his hostile older brother, were being systematically driven out of him. I saw at last that there had been something uniquely beautiful there, something unblemished by the tawdriness around him. If this cruel career went on much longer, that part of him would surely be destroyed.

"I want my supper," he said as soon as they entered the room, his gaze moving sulkily over to me. "So where is it? Get moving, Sam. I'm hungry."

Fortunately we had planned ahead and ordered dinner early that afternoon from room service, which in this hotel took two hours to send up a glass of water. I looked at my watch. "Keep calm, Humphrey," I said. "It'll be here any minute now. We already ordered all your favorite things."

"You did?" said Humphrey, leaning forward eagerly. "You mean cheeseburgers and Coke? Is that what you got?"

"Just wait and see," I said nastily. For there were no

cheeseburgers on the menu here, and I had ordered the kind of rich and highly seasoned food that Humphrey most detested: A pork and garlic sausage and sauerkraut stew, with sour cream and hot Hungarian paprika. Humphrey's face fell when he saw it. But after pausing to swear obscenely at me—which he had never done before, though he had heard the words from me often enough— he did gobble down his dinner with abandon.

It probably wasn't necessary to drug him that night, since he was already so exhausted. Still, Bridget didn't want to take any chances and had convinced him to take a "vitamin" pill before dinner. It was necessary that he discover the three new pieces as soon as possible. That night he didn't have a chance to come up with any more macabre remarks. All he did was mumble something about an island before he fell asleep on the floor with his mouth still full of food. Luc and I literally had to drag him down the hall to our room. The bumping and squeaking of his feet on the linoleum were probably audible throughout most of the hotel.

The next day I took a well-earned break from composing and went with Humphrey and Luc to the rehearsal studio, since I was mildly curious to hear what my physiologically-inspired pieces actually sounded like. I didn't stay for long. For an endless half-hour I watched Humphrey pick his way painfully through the first short Prelude, while Luc alternately hung over his shoulder and paced. Humphrey's forehead was gleaming with perspiration by the time he had finished, and I could just imagine what the warm and slippery keyboard felt like. As usual, Humphrey's first reading of the piece was so sluggish and awkward that one barely sensed any connection between the chords. Nevertheless, I had noticed a glaring wrong note toward the end, which Luc had missed. I went and stood behind Humphrey, then reached over and touched the page. "I thought that sounded funny," I said. "Look, that has to be an E flat, not a D natural."

"Oh, yeah?" Humphrey said. "Well, it looks like a D natural to me."

"But it can't be a D natural, it just sounds all wrong. And anyway, the note *does* go over the line, see?"

"Play it, Humphrey," said Luc, who was leaning over his other shoulder.

Humphrey slowly groped out the chord, playing the D natural.

"See? It sounds all wrong that way," I said.

"Not to me it doesn't," said Humphrey.

"But Humphrey, can't you hear? It's obviously an E flat," I insisted.

Luc was trying to say something, but we ignored him.

"And *I* say it's a D natural," declared Humphrey, banging out the ridiculous chord again to emphasize his point.

"You're all wet, Humphrey. It makes no musical sense that way."

"Who asked you?" Humphrey said, his voice rising. "What do you know about it, anyway?"

"I can see the music, can't I?" I slapped the page. "I can hear." I pulled on Humphrey's ear lobe. "Anybody with half an ear would know that *has* to be an E flat!"

"Oh, leave me alone! I'm sick of everybody telling me what to do!" cried Humphrey, smashing both fists down on the keyboard and leaving them there, so that the ugly jumble of notes continued to bounce around the walls of the stifling room as he shouted at me. "Who said you could come along, anyway? We don't need you. Why should anybody listen to you? You're a musical failure. Just keep your ugly little face out of it. I'm the one that wrote this music."

"Oh, yeah, Humphrey?" I said, nodding at him as I took a slow backward step. "How very pretty and flattering for you. Except that maybe there're a few ugly little secrets that you and all your devoted fans don't know anything about."

"What do you mean?" demanded Humphrey. "What are you talking about?"

Then I caught sight of Luc standing behind him, frantically shaking his head at me. He was terrified. It made me think of the last time I had suggested to Humphrey that he might not know everything, and the fear I had noticed in Bridget's voice . . .

In the midst of my bitterness and rage, I felt a sudden unexpected sweep of power. Bridget and Luc were at my mercy. Humphrey's whole rotten career was at my mercy. Why hadn't I ever seen it that way before?

"He doesn't mean anything, Humphrey. He's making it up. Aren't you, Sam?" Luc was babbling. "He's just teasing you, Humphrey, that's all. Isn't that right, Sam?"

The part of me that was still functioning rationally bit back the words I longed so much to spew at Humphrey. I knew a lot was at stake, that I had to be in control, that a rash move might be a blunder. But I was simmering with power. Still, instead of using it all up in one destructive blast, perhaps I could play around with it a little.

"I . . . uh . . ." I closed my eyes for a second, then attempted to smile. "Yes, I was just teasing you, Humphrey, that's all. I didn't mean anything. But I'm still concerned about that note." I caught Luc's eye and stared hard at him. "Considering what *you* know about Magyar's pieces, Luc, and what *I* could tell Humphrey, I'd like to hear your opinion about this note."

Luc's forehead was as damp as Humphrey's now. He bent over the page, then looked back uncomfortably at me for an instant. He cleared his throat. "Well, uh, Humphrey, I'm afraid it is the way Sam says it is. It's clearly over the—"

"But I wrote it, and I say it's a D!" bellowed Humphrey, squeezing his eyes shut and clenching his fists. "You let me play it that way or I won't practice another minute. I'm *tired* of practicing."

"He's all yours, Luc," I said. "Just remember, my discretion is in your hands. I'll be listening for that note." I grabbed my jacket, and at the door I turned back to them with a big grin. "Have just a *marvelous* day, you two. I think I might wander over to the zoo or else see what kind of movies they have around here. See you later."

And for the next day or two, I enjoyed myself. So what if I had passively allowed Bridget to walk all over me? So what if Humphrey was getting all the credit for my compositions, and I was given only insults and rejection in return? I had the power, however belatedly discovered, to put an end to the whole situation. All I had to do was tell Humphrey everything. This power gave a certain unreality to all their frantic hurryings and scurryings and allowed me to feel competent and in control as I watched them. I amused myself by frightening Luc a few more times, but I didn't try it on Bridget. You had to be careful with her. She was too smart to play games with unless you planned them out very carefully.

So I had my fun with Luc and felt almost immune to Humphrey's increasingly virulent insults. I especially enjoyed writing my next Magyar piece, a Ballade inspired by the tirelessly inventive hotel radiators. All in all, things seemed to be looking up.

Until the night before Humphrey's opening Vienna concert, when I walked into our room and found a bundle wrapped in rags lying on his bed.

9

FOR A MOMENT I couldn't put the picture together. There was something too incongruous about the stained and stiffened package fouling the white pillowcase. Then I remembered Magyar's death and the game of twenty questions and the old man's latest cryptic observation, and my guts turned over. There was an unpleasant, swinish grunt, not even remotely recognizable as my own voice. I gulped violently, feeling as though I had just staggered off a roller coaster. But almost at once a sudden rush of hostility stepped in like an invigorating drug. My weakness vanished. Without thinking I spun around and stormed back down the hall to their room.

. Because Humphrey would be performing every night for the next week, tonight was our last chance to dope him and introduce a new Magyar piece. Bridget had already slipped him the pill in a glass of Coke, and now they were waiting for room service to deliver up some of its rancid swill. The poor things were sadly disappointed when they saw that it was only me at the door. And Humphrey was already in a rotten mood because his practice schedule hadn't allowed him to eat all day.

"All right, who's the joker?" I demanded.

They didn't even bother to answer me.

"Come on! Who left the little surprise package on Humphrey's bed?"

Bridget sighed. "Oh, Sam, *now* what are you—"

"Just come with me," I ordered. "There's something very cute I want all of you to see."

My tone of voice compelled even sullen, quarrelsome Humphrey to haul his bulk down the corridor. I ushered them into the room and gestured at the bed. "All right, 'fess up," I said.

"Sam, what *is* all this fuss about?" Bridget was genuinely baffled.

"Are you blind? I'm talking about that charming object on Humphrey's bed. Remember Magyar's precious bundle wrapped in rags?"

"But Sam, obviously one of the maids just . . ." Bridget began. Then her voice trailed off. The bundle really was quite peculiar when you took a good look at it. The fabric had that ancient, brittle quality of mummy wrappings, except that mummy wrappings are plain, and these rags, though faded now, had once been bright and garish prints. The stains upon them, rather than being reminiscent of mere dirt and grease, somehow gave the impression that they were the result of fetid and purulent oozings. It was not the most attractive bit of gift wrapping. There was also an oddly familiar bitter medicinal smell about the thing, which was now beginning to permeate the room.

"Come now, Sam," Bridget said, with a withering little laugh. "You don't really think those cleaning rags have anything to do with that story about Magyar's bundle, do you? It's simply too farfetched."

"That all depends on what's inside," I told her. "Care to have a peek?"

Humphrey had been doped only five minutes before, so there hadn't yet been time for the drug to have its weird effect on him. It usually took almost an hour. He belched petulantly. "Will somebody tell me what this is all about?" he complained. "What 'bundle'? I don't know what you're talking about. I never heard of any bundle."

"That's very odd, isn't it, Humphrey?" I said. "Since it was *you* who brought it up last week when we played twenty questions. You acted like two human hands wrapped in rags was the funniest thing you ever heard of. How could you forget it?"

"*I* brought it up?" he said blankly. "No, I didn't. You're just making it up."

Bridget and Luc exchanged a glance. And I knew that the coincidences were finally beginning to get through even to Bridget when she turned on me and said, "You put it there, didn't you, Sam?"

"Me?" I was astonished. "Come on, now. I'm the last person who would do that. I'm the one who's been so 'neurotic' about the whole thing, to use your word. Why would I want to make it any worse?"

She gave me a hard stare and then turned away, puzzled. I was a good liar to everyone but Bridget, who could always see through me. She knew I was telling the truth.

"Did I *really* say that last week?" Humphrey whined. "Sam's making it up, isn't he?"

"You said it, Humphrey," I told him. Bridget did not contradict me.

I could see his face begin to screw up the way it did when he was going to throw a tantrum—a technique he had discovered only in the last few weeks. "But the night we played that game, that was the time I composed in Geneva, wasn't it?" He looked around belligerently at us. We nodded. "Well, that's why I don't remember. I never remember very much about it. And it wasn't even *me* who talked about the bundle, it was Magyar. He made me say it. That's the explanation. He knew we were going to find it here, so he made me say something about it ahead of time." He glanced around at us again. "Well? How come you still look so funny? Isn't that the explanation?"

Not surprisingly, for a moment no one came up with a response. Then I said, looking directly at Bridget, "Sure, it's a great explanation. Isn't it, Bridget? Of course it was *only* Magyar's ghost all along. That solves the whole problem, doesn't it?"

"Oh, shut up, Sam," Bridget said.

"Don't act like I'm stupid! What's wrong with my explanation?" Humphrey asked, more annoyed now.

"Nothing, if you like going to sleep with two human hands on your pillow," I said. "Don't you want to unwrap your little present and see what's inside, Humf?"

Humphrey scowled, but didn't respond. We all just stood and looked at the repulsive object. No one said a word.

Until I couldn't stand it any longer and darted over to the bed. "Well I do," I said, and reached toward the pillow.

"Sam, don't!" Bridget cried shrilly.

I froze, my arm extended, my eyes on her.

"Call the maid. Get her to come and take it away," said Bridget.

"That'll take days." Then I smiled at her. "Bridget, I'm surprised at you. Aren't you even curious? After all, you told me yourself there's *nothing* to be alarmed about. We can't just leave this thing here, you know."

"But . . ." Bridget said, biting her lip.

"I'm looking," I said. I held my breath and reached out toward the mildewed fabric. Gingerly, I pulled at a piece of cloth with thumb and forefinger. It felt revoltingly moist, like someone else's used handkerchief. The cloth fell away, but there were others underneath, still hiding whatever was wrapped inside. With sudden impatience I picked up the entire bundle with my fist and shook it out.

Two hands tumbled out onto the bed.

Luc, his face pasty, sank down into a chair. Bridget choked and pressed her hand to her throat.

The hands on the bed were about an inch long. Though chipped and cracked, they were still intact enough to make the primitive style of the carving immediately apparent. The doll from which they had been amputated must have been quite old and very likely handmade as well.

Bridget began laughing gaily.

"What's so funny?" Humphrey said. His imminent-tantrum expression intensified.

"Oh, it was just . . . just such a relief," said Bridget, with one last delicate peal. "I mean . . . for a moment I was actually afraid there *might* be a real pair of hands in there. I can't imagine what made me so silly. And now, it's kind of a relief to see we really had nothing to worry about, after all."

I gaped at her. What an awesome phenomenon she was! Let's say she had decided to deny the existence of elephants. And then I dropped one from a tenth story window to land one inch away from her on the sidewalk. She'd walk right past that squashed mountain without a flicker of an eyelash or a break in her conversation. All she had to do was choose not to see it.

" 'Nothing to worry about?' " I repeated stupidly. The situation was so obvious to me that I couldn't imagine someone else not seeing it, and consequently I had difficulty even finding the words to explain it. "I mean . . . okay, so it's not real hands, but . . . but it still means somebody knows more than we think. They even know what we talk about in our room! And they're trying to scare us, or stop us, or something." I gestured at the little hands on the bed. "Why do something weird like this, if they're not trying to tell us something? Can't you see? They know what Humphrey said last week. And they know everything else, too!"

"You're overwrought, Sam. We all are. You'll feel better when—"

"What do you mean, they know everything?" Humphrey asked, his voice rising.

I ignored both of them. "They *are* trying to tell us something, and we better listen. They know exactly what we're doing, they could *expose* us. It's like blackmail. I swear, they're going to expose us if we don't—"

"Watch it, Sam!" said Bridget, hissing out my name like a venomous snake.

Luc was on his feet, tugging at Humphrey's arm. "Come on, Humphrey, we'd better get back to our room in case the food arrives," he pleaded.

But Humphrey was angry and curious enough now even to resist the lure of food. "What do you mean, 'expose us,' Sam? I want to know. Tell me this minute!"

"Sam doesn't really know *what* he means, Humphrey dear," Bridget explained, her mouth twisting with contempt. "He doesn't even know what he's saying. I had *hoped* he wasn't too envious and weak-minded to deal with this excitement, but I'm afraid my hopes have proved to be unjustified. You were right, Luc. He's cracked. It's what's called a mental breakdown, Humphrey. I see we're going to have to send him away somewhere, where he can rest. But for the moment, all we can do is leave him alone so he can calm his sick nerves." She pulled the hotel keys, which she always kept, out of the pocket of her suit jacket. "Fortunately, these doors can be double-locked from the outside—"

She went on talking when Humphrey interrupted her, but it was useless because his voice was powerful with animosity now. "All right, all right, so Sam's a little feeble in the head, so he can't take it when people pay attention to all my talents. Don't you think I already *knew* how pitiful and jealous he was? But I still want to know what he means by 'expose' and 'blackmail.'" He twisted away from Luc and in two heavy steps was posed threateningly above me, staring down with hot little eyes. "Tell me, Sam," he demanded, "or I'll stuff those stinking rags down your ugly mouth."

That was all the encouragement I needed. "With pleasure, Humphrey," I said without hesitation, taking care to speak clearly and distinctly. "There is no such thing as Magyar's ghost. It's all a hoax. Not only do you have no musical talent, Humphrey, but you have no psychic talent either. The whole thing was made up, invented. Let me tell you why."

"Sam!" Bridget shrieked.

"You grew too big, Humphrey, and people stopped coming to your concerts, remember? We protected you from the truth, then. We didn't read you all the well-deserved rotten reviews. But the reason they stopped coming was because you have no talent. Sure, you can play the notes, but there's more to it than that, something called making music, and that's beyond you, Humphrey. When you were little and cute it didn't matter, they came to see a freak; but when you got big they stopped coming, because they saw that you weren't even the shadow of an excuse for a real pianist. Most parents would have given up at that point and stopped pushing you on stage, tried to give you a normal life. But not your saintly devoted mother. She couldn't bear saying goodbye to all that lovely acclaim you'd been earning for her. So she came up with a plan. Here's how it works, Humf . . ."

Of course, while I was saying all this, Bridget and Luc were hardly just standing there contemplating my choice of words. They were quite busy. Luc had redoubled his efforts to get Humphrey out of the room, hugging his waist like a football tackle and trying to drag him backwards. But Humphrey stood his ground, mesmerized by my voice, swatting back at Luc as if he were an annoying insect. Bridget concentrated on me, clawing at my mouth and kicking out at my shins with her pointed high heels. Small as I was, however, I was bigger than Bridget, and I managed to keep her at arm's length most of the time. The words continued to flow relentlessly from my mouth like a mindless unstoppable recording, impeded only by an occasional grunt or gasp of pain.

". . . First of all, *I* compose the Magyar pieces, Humphrey, with my own conscious brain and no supernatural assistance. Pitiful, jealous Sam, the musical failure, is the one who writes the music your fans think is so brilliant and convincing. And then we drug you, Humf, we dissolve a powerful sleeping pill in your Coke. And that knocks you out and makes you forget things. We arrange you at the desk with *my* music, and we slip a pen into your fat hand, and that's it. All we had to do was make a few little suggestions, and you fell for it like a cement balloon. I wasn't sure you were simpleminded enough, but Bridget was. You're just the fake façade, Humphrey, the front, the empty—"

Then I shrieked. Bridget was chewing on my hand with her sharp little rodent teeth. I bent over and butted her in the midriff with my head. She wilted and collapsed onto the bed. And Luc, as if his current had been cut off, staggered away from Humphrey to sag against the wall.

Humphrey and I still stood facing each other. Luc and Bridget were too busy fighting for breath to be able to speak. In the next room, someone was doing a meticulous and juicy job of blowing his nose, in G major.

"I . . . it's a lie, isn't it?" Humphrey said weakly.

"Not on your life, Humphrey," I said.

"It's a lie, it's a lie, I know it is!" he shouted, turning first to Bridget, then to Luc.

Slowly Luc straightened up, making an effort to pull himself together. "Uh . . . certainly it's a lie," he said. "Don't . . . pay any attention to any of that. It's all . . . just lies."

But it was such a hopelessly feeble denial that even Humphrey could only interpret it as an affirmation of everything I had said. "But why . . . how could . . ." Humphrey stammered. His face was becoming violently pink. "I just don't understand how you . . . It just doesn't . . ."

As I watched him struggling to make sense of it all, profoundly shaken, bewildered and helpless and hurt, something shifted inside of me. I stepped toward him. "Humphrey," I said, "don't take it like that, please. I didn't know what I . . ."

He pivoted, and faster than I had ever seen him move, he fled from the room.

Then Luc smacked me hard on the face. I was too stunned to protect myself. "You dirty rotten perverted little swine," he snarled, forcing me back against the wall. "You loathsome stinking piece of filth." I had never heard him so articulate. "Do you know what you've done? Do you have any idea what effect your selfishness could have on him? Do you?" He hit me again. "Do you?"

Bridget, meanwhile, had recovered enough to drag herself off the bed and shut the door. "Stop it, Luc, someone will hear you," she said, concerned with appearances even in the midst of calamity. "They've already heard too much."

"But he has to be punished. He has to be made to understand what a terrible thing he's done."

"All in good time," she said, shakily pushing her braids back into place. "He will be richly and exactingly punished, be assured of that. But first, he has one final duty to perform. He is coming back with us to *convince* Humphrey that everything he just said was a lie."

"But how can he—" Luc began.

"He'll find a way. If it is necessary to grovel on his belly and lick Humphrey's boots, he'll do it. *Now.*"

They each grabbed me by an arm and began maneuvering me toward the door. "I'll do it, I'll do it. Just keep your hands off," I said, wriggling away from them. "I tell you, I'll *do* it. I want to get it over with as much as you do."

I meant it. The three of us hurried down the hall. "I must have forgotten to lock the door," Bridget muttered inanely as we herded together into their room.

The room was empty.

"Humphrey!" Bridget wailed, for a moment actually out of control. Luc headed for the tiny closet, and I sped off down the length of the hallway. There were dirty greenish walls and lots of closed doors, but no Humphrey. The dial over the elevator indicated that it had stopped in the lobby.

"Nothing," I announced, coming back into the room. "He's not out there."

"But this . . . it's impossible," Luc said. "He's never done anything like this before."

"He's never been maimed like this before," Bridget said, grabbing a cigarette. "If this mess has any serious effect on him, Sam, I promise you you'll regret it to your dying day."

"If you'd stop making threats and start thinking, we might be able to find him," I said.

"But this is just so unlike him," Luc said uselessly.

"We're wasting time," I said. "We should be combing the place. There's a chance he's still somewhere inside the hotel."

"*Inside the hotel!*" Luc moaned, wringing his hands. "You don't think he could have *run away?*"

"How the hell do *I* know what he did?" I was shouting now. "We have to start looking!"

There was a knock on the door.

"Oh, there he is, thank *God!*" cried Bridget, pushing me out of the way. "I thought you said he wasn't out there, Sam," she shot back at me. "Great eyes you have." She pulled open the door.

"You dinner, pliz?" said the decrepit waiter, and he wheeled the trembling little white-covered table into the room. "Yes? This right room?" he asked, looking around at us, when we didn't say anything.

"Uh, sure," I said.

It was the same waiter who had brought us food several times before. "Yes, that what I think." He nodded. "Only but on my way up I see other young man go out, and I wonder if—"

"The other young man? You saw him? Where?" Bridget demanded, darting forward to grab the waiter's upper arm.

"Oh, yes, sure and in such hurry," the waiter said,

smiling. "Out lift door zoom, like cannon. I think maybe he late for concert, and maybe you no want food. But you want, yes?"

In a flash, Bridget had rallied in that uncanny way of hers. Brisk and businesslike, she thrust a bill into the waiter's hand and hustled him to the door. "Thank you, thank you very much," she said and pushed him out of the room. Then she swung back to face me.

"What are we waiting for?" I said. "We've got to get out there and find him!"

"*We* do, Sam, but not you."

"Don't be stupid! The more people looking, the better our chances are."

"Others will help, but not you. You are not to be trusted. You are never to be trusted again."

"But . . ."

"Get your coat, Luc!" she barked. He rushed to the door.

"But you're crazy!" I said. "You can't stop me from looking!"

She held up the key. "It can be locked from the outside," she reminded me. "You are staying safe and sound in this room, where you can't do any more damage, until we find him and bring him back. And if you get bored, you can while away the time trying to imagine what I am going to do to you when I return. Goodbye, Sam."

Then they were outside, and I heard the key turning in the lock. I threw myself against the door, but it was too late. "You can't do this!" I screamed and pounded on the door. It didn't budge. I buried my head in my hands and sank slowly to the linoleum.

It was unbearable to be locked away like a naughty

135

child, forced to do nothing when the situation was so desperate. Humphrey was alone in a foreign city, for the first time in his life. It was night. It had never occurred to him to look at a map; he would be lost a block away from the hotel. He had no money. He knew nothing of the language. He had no experience in *any* language in asking directions or help from passersby. He was hopelessly gullible and naive, as fragile and defenseless as a baby.

To make it worse, he was entering this situation in a state of mindless, hysterical panic. The most important things in his life had just been brutally torn away from him. He would probably run blindly until he was exhausted and not realize until then that he had cut himself off from everything he knew, from anyone who could help him. How would he feel then? What would he do? What might be done to him? The possibilities were unlimited.

The final touch, the frosting on the cake, was the pill he had been slipped, which at any minute would begin taking effect.

When that little detail hit me, I groaned aloud. It didn't bear thinking about; it was too terrible to be real. My mind curled and shrivelled away from the thought like cellophane dropped into a fire.

Indeed, something inside me had changed. It had begun as soon as I had spewed out my last revelation at Humphrey. My sadistic truth-telling had been the key, the catalyst that had set off this startling internal reaction. Perhaps there might have been a less destructive way to unleash the transformation, perhaps this was the only way, I didn't know. What I did know was that suddenly, and for the first time, I was aware of how much I loved him.

I loved Humphrey. He was probably the only person in the world I did love. Tenderness I hadn't known was possible welled up in me. Yet I had just hurt him so terribly that there was a good chance he might not survive it.

And where was I now, when he needed me more than he ever had? I was locked up in a crummy hotel room with four stinking platters of *szelekey gulyas*.

10

THERE HAD to be a way to get out.

There was little floor space in the small dreary room, but I managed to pace, wrangling feverishly over the limited possibilities. The making-a-rope-out-of-bedsheets gambit occurred to me, but when I peeped out of the sixth story window I discarded it. Swashbuckling was hardly my style. I considered shrieking and banging on the door until someone came with a key to make me shut up. But that tactic would draw unwanted public attention to our sordid situation. What about picking the lock? Bridget had plenty of large hairpins and nail files. For a time I crouched by the door, poking bits of metal into the crack and the keyhole with clumsy, sweating fingers. But when one of the hairpins broke off in the space between the door and the wall I stopped. If something got wedged into the keyhole, they'd have to remove the entire door to get me out, and it would probably be days before they got around to doing that. I resumed pacing. The ugly furniture crowded around me. I looked out the window again. I kicked the door a couple of times. I paced.

And all the time I was thinking of Humphrey, passed out in a gutter with rats, stripped of his American clothes by starving derelicts, dying of pneumonia in a garbage-strewn alley. I thought of the misery he must be feeling, the devastation so bottomless it could hardly be imagined. What reason did he really have to try to find his way back? What was there to prevent him from throwing himself off a bridge into the murk? Not only had I deprived him of all self-respect, I had also taken his family away from him. He would see himself as utterly betrayed by the only people he cared about, a spiritual orphan. Why would he want to go on living at all?

I puffed furiously at one of Bridget's cigarettes, but it only made me feel sick. I stomped around the little portable table. The sight of those piles of cold sour meat, swimming in thickly congealed fat, intensified my nausea. If someone didn't get them out of here soon, I would puke. Without thinking, I picked up the phone to call room service.

Only then did the simple, obvious solution hit me. I had been too upset to see straight. How much time had I already wasted?

I dialed the desk. The phone buzzed and buzzed in my ear in F sharp. No one answered. I let it go on ringing, studying the minute hand on my watch. It was now 10:15. How long ago had Humphrey run away? I had no idea. I brutally ground my teeth, tapped my foot, cracked my knuckles. The phone continued to buzz futilely. Had everyone in the hotel taken the night off?

Then at last the meaningless guttural syllables came bleating out of the earpiece.

"Please, do you speak English?" I demanded.

"Uh . . . no . . . uh."

"Hurry, find someone, please!" I screamed. "This is an emergency."

Mutterings and thumps, thumps and mutterings. Hadn't the dope noticed the urgency in my voice? I looked at my watch. It was already 10:25.

"Yes. What you want?"

"Listen, please, this is an emergency," I said, as slowly and distinctly as I could manage. "I have accidentally been locked in my parents' room. I have no key. I *must* get out. Could you please send someone up as quickly as possible to unlock the door. It's room 1056."

"What is you say?" The voice was bored. "I no understand."

"I am locked in room 1056," I repeated, my knuckles whitening as I gripped the receiver. "Someone must come to let me out."

"Locked in room? I no understand. How is that happen?"

"That doesn't matter! It was an accident. I *must* get out quickly. Please send someone up as fast as possible. The number is 1056."

"Yes, but all very busy now." The voice was maddeningly calm. "I do not know when someone may come."

"But this is an *emergency*. Don't you understand? You must come right away, because . . . uh, I am sick," I improvised. "I am very sick, get it? I must use the toilet. If I stay here, I will make a big mess. I will be sick all over the room. It will be very dirty, very smelly and dirty."

"What is room number?" he said, prodded to action at last by the thought of vomit stains on the linoleum.

"1056. And hurry." I gagged throatily at him and hung up.

Apparently Bridget had not left instructions at the desk to keep me locked up. At another time she might well have come up with a convincing explanation for such an unusual request. Tonight she must have been too rushed to be sufficiently inventive—and knew that that instruction would only stir up more curiosity. She had probably been hoping I would be too stupid to think of the obvious, and she had almost been right.

I waited. The minutes limped along. By the time someone did knock on the door, a quarter of an hour later, it certainly would have been too late to protect the linoleum.

"Is someone?" came a cracked voice.

"Yes, right here!" I called, pounding on the door in response. "Please let me out."

I heard heavy breathing and keys jangling sluggishly. Then my rescuer began to hum, a miserable wavering drone that slipped gradually from one key to another, remaining always noxiously out of tune. The barely discernible melody almost sounded like my own composition, "Yeller Gal," but of course that was ridiculous. "You've got to hurry," I pleaded and banged on the door again to try to shut him up. But the humming went obliviously on, as though the situation were merely routine, as though people in Vienna were always locking one another up in hotel rooms, and it was one of his nightly duties to go around setting them free.

"Oh, I feel so sick," I loudly moaned. "In a minute I'll be sick over the floor."

And in a minute I nearly was. For when the door opened at last, standing there with a bunch of keys and a big grin was my familiar friend, the little old man.

11

I STAGGERED backwards away from him as if he had pushed me. Delicate sounds came out of my mouth. Then my rear end made contact with the room service cart.

I spun around to see it career into the bedside table. The plates made a lot of noise piling up at the far end, and one of them threatened to tip off onto the bed. I grabbed for it, protecting the bed but bathing my hand in fatty sauce. The closest thing to a towel that I could see was the white tablecloth. As I hastily made use of it I kept looking back at the little old man, blushing. I felt so foolish that I almost forgot how frightened I was. "What are *you* doing here?" I said, shaking my head.

He tottered closer, bending forward at the waist and cupping an ear with his hand. "Please, I not hear you," he said, his accent so thick that "hear" sounded almost like "cheer."

I couldn't seem to get the grease off my fingers, perhaps because the tablecloth was already so greasy. "Who are you, anyway?" I muttered.

"Ah!" He nodded merrily. "I understand. Whoo.

AM. I." He pointed at his chest and lifted his bushy eyebrows. He did have hands, after all. But he was so shrunken with age that they barely emerged from the sleeves of the threadbare black coat he wore, which was nipped in at the waist in turn of the century style. Underneath it he had on a heavy dull green workshirt. Stained brownish trousers bagged around his ankles and hung loose at his waist, supported by a pair of black suspenders. Matted white hair brushed against his shoulders as he continued to nod at me. "Yessss. Who. AM. I," he repeated playfully. "You will be interest to know."

"I don't have time for games now," I said, made aggressive by fear. "My brother—and *you* know who he is—is lost. He will be hurt. I must find him." As I passed him on the way to the door, I noticed a familiar medicinal smell. I had the horrible sensation that I was letting the solution to everything slip through my fingers, yet how could I stop to interrogate him now? "Please, could you just wait here?" I said, turning back to him from the door. "There is so much I have to find out, but I just *can't* right now. Wait here, please."

"No! Stop! Wait!" He held up his trembling clawlike hand and waved frantically at me. "You listen, pliz."

"But I just *can't!*" I turned to go.

"But you brother. He is . . . I got," I heard him croak behind me. "I got brother. You see? I got."

"*What?*" I spun back into the room and grabbed his bony shoulders. "What do you mean, you got? Do you know where he is?"

"Yeh, yeh, sure." From this close I could see the crusty skull beneath his thin hair, and I perceived that

144

he was not nodding, but that his head was merely quivering with palsy. And yet there was an alertness in his gray and yellow eyes that belied the outward appearances of senility. "I got brother, sure. He so . . . how you say? . . . So, tired, so tired. Yeh. He sleep now."

"But where?" I seemed to be shaking him. Did he really know what he was talking about? Could I take the risk of believing him? "How is he? Is he all right? Where did you leave him?"

"Stop it! You hurting me." He twitched his shoulders away from my hands, and his chin jutted out petulantly above the wattles on his neck. "Must be . . . sweet, or you break me. I helping. Is not sweet break me." He was having some difficulty breathing. I must have been shaking him harder than I realized.

"Oh, all right, I'm sorry, I didn't mean to hurt you." I whined at him like a fretful child. The situation had the stubborn unreality of a nightmare. I could find no firm footing, no basis for the safety of rationality. "I'm confused, I don't know what . . ." Now my hands were shaking too. "Is Humphrey all right? Can you take me to him?"

"Take you? Well, but of course it is, yes." Good humored once more, he bowed at me, a gracious, formal gesture. "Of course I take. If you give me answers. Why you think I come? I got plenty questions ask."

I'll bet you do, I thought, "Well, come on then, let's go," I said, more impatient than ever now. For it had struck me that at any moment Bridget or Luc might come back. I was in no mood to be locked up again. Later on, I would decide how much to tell the old man.

I raced ahead of him down the hall and pounded on the elevator button. I continued pounding it pointlessly as the obtuse contraption paused for a leisurely sojourn on every floor—it was the only elevator in the hotel and usually crowded. Not until it was on its way from nine to ten did it occur to me that Bridget or Luc might be on it. As the doors shuddered and began to open, I pressed myself back against the wall. The old man looked at me curiously. "We go, yeh?" he said. No one emerged, so I pushed him gently ahead of me and stepped inside.

There were five other people in the elevator, which was still on its way up. I discourteously pushed the lobby button, but the obstinate machine clung to its original course and creaked up to the twelfth floor. People got on and off. When we returned to the tenth floor, I hid behind them, in the unlikely event that Bridget or Luc had gone up the stairs and found the room empty. No one got on. Then the old man began to hum, and I forgot all about them.

I listened carefully. It was "Yeller Gal," there was no doubt about it. "What are you humming?" I asked him softly, so the others wouldn't hear, as we stopped on three.

He put his hand up to his ear. "Yeh? What you say?"

"That music that you are humming," I said more distinctly. "What is it?"

He shrugged and smiled. "Ah, but who know? I . . . how you say, hum? Hummmm?" He laughed. "I *hummmmm* many music. You know this music I am *hummmm*?" He laughed again. The word amused him.

We were heading toward two now. "Yes, I do know," I said. "It was one of Humphrey's new Magyar pieces. The first one he played."

But he didn't understand, and I had to repeat myself. He still didn't understand. Finally I had to hum it, directly into his ear. The elevator was so packed with people now that no one paid much attention to us.

We had almost reached the lobby. "Oh, *that* one!" he said. "Yeh, sure I know well." He tilted his head to the side and pursed his lips. "Is sweet, yeh? Is a sweet one. Nice to *hummmm*."

"But how did you know . . ." I began. The doors opened. In the rude push to get out I didn't have a chance to finish the question. Since the impatient people outside in the lobby didn't have the decency to wait until the elevator was empty, quite a seething melee ensued as the two groups met at the threshold. Several people had wedged in between me and the old man, so I kept my eyes on him instead of my immediate vicinity as we inched forward. Then some obnoxious person getting on actually had the gall to elbow me hard in the ribs. I turned aside to see who it was and make a nasty remark.

Bridget and I recognized each other at the same moment.

"Sam!" she cried shrilly. "Where the hell do you think you're going?"

I flinched, feeling her power. "With . . . with him," I said, pointing at the little old man.

"Who the hell is he?" she demanded, taking a good look at him. Then she grabbed me. "Get in here!" The crowd kept moving, pushing us back into the elevator.

I almost gave in. If I had been running away on my own, her command might well have drawn me back. But for once I wasn't thinking of myself. Helping Humphrey was all that mattered. And Bridget didn't want to help him; she wanted to make sure he didn't miss his concert tomorrow. I had to get to him first—and the determination to do so gave me the strength to resist her.

I didn't even have to think. With both hands I shoved Bridget as hard as I could into the elevator. She staggered backwards, ricocheted against the back wall and started toward me. But the people on either side of me surged forward then and hemmed her in. I squeezed violently through them in the opposite direction, flailing my elbows, kicking out with my feet. In a moment the bottleneck was behind me.

The old man had been watching. "But where she go?" he asked plaintively. "She no want come? We wait, yeh?"

"No!" I grabbed his elbow and started for the main entrance. "We have to get away before she gets out of there."

"But . . . I no understand." I was going more slowly than I wanted, but it was nevertheless a struggle for him to keep up with me. I continued to pull him relentlessly across the lobby. 'Stop! I can no keep! We wait, I am give dicatate!"

"No!" I glanced back quickly. The elevator doors were just beginning to move together at last. I could see a struggle going on toward the back of the car, several people seemed to have fallen down and there were yelps of outrage, but the front line held and the doors slid shut before anyone spilled out. It would be a while now before Bridget could battle her way out of there. I slowed down just a bit.

The old man was gasping for breath now. "Stop! I give dicatate!" he pleaded.

I pushed open the hotel door and dragged him past the lighted entrance and down the block to a shadowy alley. There I allowed him to lean against the wall and painfully catch his breath. It was several minutes before he was able to speak.

"Is trouble?" he said at last.

"You noticed," I said. I was feeling a little better now, having escaped Bridget, but I was still impatient to get away from the hotel as fast as possible. "Can you take me to Humphrey now? Which way?"

He pushed himself feebly away from the wall. "Well. Is direction," he said, starting back toward the hotel entrance.

"No, not that way! We must stay hidden, so they won't see us. We must go another way."

It took a few more tries before I got the idea across to him. Then he shook his head irritably and muttered something, but he did start off down the alley. After a few steps we both looked at each other and started to speak at the same time.

"Why Humpy is running?" he said.

"How did you get those keys?" I said.

"Pardon."

"Excuse me."

"Why—"

"How—"

He stopped for a moment to chuckle. I glanced back down the alley, but so far no one was pursuing us. I still wasn't sure I really believed that the old man knew where Humphrey was. Still, now that I had had a chance to think about it, I couldn't see any reason not to go with him. My only alternative was to wander around aimlessly by myself, a pretty hopeless plan considering the size of Vienna. This path was as good as any random one I might take, and it had the added advantage that the old man might turn out to have Humphrey after all. Not to mention the fact that I had some questions to ask him.

"Go on, you first," I said graciously.

"Why Humpy is running tonight?" he repeated, starting to walk again.

"It's a long story, I'll tell you later," I said ungraciously. "But first, how did *you* find him, anyway?"

"I am waiting for him, of course. I have many questions."

"You were waiting for him?" We had reached the street at the other end of the alley. His face was visible again in the glow of a streetlight, and I could clearly see his complacent grin as he smugly met my eye. "How could you be waiting for him? You didn't know he was going to run away."

"No, of course." He shrugged. "But still I wait and hope to see. Very important talk, yeh?" He winked with arch significance, then hobbled off to the left.

I followed. Now that the escape seemed to be behind us, and I had the opportunity to think, my previous dread of him began trickling back. I suppressed the impulse to demand how much he knew about us. I wasn't ready for that yet. "But what did you say to him? What happened?" I still wasn't sure I should believe him. "How did you get him to go with you?"

"I am in lobby waiting. I see him go *vivace* out of . . . how you say? . . . Ah, yeh, out of *lift*. He is too much speed for see me or listen to me or make stop. So . . ." He giggled. "So I go put myself direct in front and is collision, *molto* collision, and we both then on floor."

I was impressed by the physical recklessness of the old guy, casting himself in Humphrey's path like a toreador confronting a colossal bull. "But what did you do then?" I asked him. "How did you keep Humphrey from just getting up again and running away?"

"Ah, yeh, yeh. I see he not listen the courtesy, the 'Pliz to wait.' So right quick, *pronto*, I tell him whoo I am."

"Tell him *what?*" I demanded, feeling a delicate movement in the hairs on the back of my neck. I glanced over my shoulder again. The lone streetlight was far behind us now, the silent stone houses obscured by thick shadows. The street was absolutely deserted. I couldn't even see a lighted window.

"Only I tell him: Whoo. I. Am. Then, he listen, yeh." He giggled again.

I could feel prickling now over my entire back and arms. "Well?" I said thickly. "Go on. Who are you?"

He turned to me with an arrogant toss of his scrawny little head. "I am only child of Laszlo Magyar, of course."

Oddly enough, my initial response to this revelation was a perverse disappointment. What kind of bizarre fantasy had I been expecting—Magyar's ghost, if not the somehow miraculously preserved composer himself? Consciously, of course not. Yet this wretchedly frail and shabby descendant, in comparison to the romantic terrors inspired by the Magyar book, struck me as something of a letdown. A lot I knew.

"Oh . . . that's amazing," I said, rather numbly. "Um, congratulations."

I didn't sound very impressed, but that didn't faze him a bit. "Yes, only child." He couldn't suppress a gentle cackle as he stared up at me. "Make Humpy think, I bet, yeh? Even if he no read book I write about father, he still look then, pay heed; he listen. I say I have plenty thing ask, tell, show. Want know about music he write. He come like babe, after. He come to home." Then he frowned. "But I no understand, he so tired, so funny, almost not walk, not can answer. He go sleep. So I come back." He grinned at me again. "You understand how I feel? I decide spill, ask. I need do it right away, *subito*. If not Humpy, then I go back, get other one spill . . . how you say? . . . Beans! I spill you beans."

"Wait a minute. *You* wrote the Magyar book?"

"Yeh, sure, why not?" There was pride in the tilt of his shoulders as he hobbled along beside me. "I like very much, book."

"So did I."

"What? *You* read?" he demanded eagerly, scrabbling at my sleeve.

"Of course I did. What do you expect?" I was finally beginning to react. All at once an army of vital questions began battling in my mind, as messily as the people pushing their way into the elevator. Chief among them: Did he know about the hoax? Did he possess information that could expose us? How did he personally feel, poor as he so obviously was, about the way we were making use of his father's name to rake in the cash? What was his opinion of the drivel we were passing off as his father's music? What were the beans he wanted to spill? Was he insane? What did he want to do with us? What *could* he do?

There was also the question of Humphrey. How much damage had I done to him? What was his state of mind when they left the hotel? And how much had he told the old man before succumbing to the drug?

Those were the really heavy ones, and I was trying to ready myself to deal with them. But there was still something that had to be swept out of the way first.

"The book was great," I said quite honestly. He beamed. "I have so many things to ask you," I went on. "But first, there's something I don't understand."

"Yeh. Tell pliz." He turned again, into a narrow unlit alley that curved to the right and descended steeply. I could not see where it led. He seemed quite familiar with the place, automatically stepping around the potholes in the slippery paving stones.

"Well, uh, first of all," I said, forced to pick my way carefully as I tried to think, "Um . . . oh, yes! How come it was *you* who came to let me out of the room? Where did you get your hands on those keys?"

He shrugged. "Only that? Is nothing. I am wait in lobby. Then Fritz give me sign. Tell me—"

"Hold on. Who's Fritz?"

"Ah, little Fritz! I know from baby. He student, I give piano teaching for many year. Is hopeless. No music inside." He pushed his finger in his scaly ear and grimaced. "So brutal he play! But sweet boy. Now *big* man at hotel, big importance behind big desk. I come sometimes and see. He give me sign and tell me is . . . How you say? . . . Is some . . . Oh, yes! Some screwball lock self in room. All boys busy. Tell me go unlet from room screwball. I want say no, if go unlet screwball, maybe lose person I wait for to spill beans. Then I think to ask name of person stay in room. I am in fortune! Is room of family to spill beans. So I go. No big deal. Is nothing."

"Yeah, but if you knew what a nightmare it was to see you there, you wouldn't say it was nothing."

"What you say? I no understand this word."

"It doesn't matter. Uh, listen . . ." I began to be aware of a foul-smelling mist, slimy against my face. It reminded me of the stinking Venetian canals. Before I had a chance to stop it, one of the questions I had been putting off until later popped out of my mouth. "That was you in Venice, wasn't it? Bridget said it couldn't be. But *were* you there, outside the stage door after Humphrey's concert?"

But he was too busy searching through his pockets to answer. We turned out of the alley, and I almost walked into the river, so narrow was the embankment. The water was hidden by mist, but I could feel the waves lapping thinly at the soles of my shoes, making limp sucking noises against the stone. "Home sweet home," my companion crooned, fumbling at an old wooden door, its threshold only inches above the level of the water.

"You live *here?*" I stepped back to get a better look at the house, and my foot was drenched. All I could tell from so close was that the building was incredibly narrow, only about ten feet wide, and four stories tall. On one side was the alley, and on the other, separated by a space of one foot, loomed a massive and featureless brick edifice that was probably a warehouse.

"Sure I live here. Why not?" The old man grunted as he pushed the door open. "Is good fortune, have own house. Pliz to enter, yeh?" He bowed and gestured me in ahead of him. I took a tentative step into cold and complete darkness. It was like walking with my eyes closed. I stopped stupidly just inside the door. The old man had to push me out of the way in order to get past.

I could hear him shuffling across the floor, bumping into things. "Is light, in moment," he muttered. I waited where I was. Seeing nothing, I became more aware than usual of odors. There was a general moldy basement smell, and above that I detected rancid grease and onions and garbage and dust, and a pervasive reek of animal urine. I was also aware of a distant whiff of that curious medicinal redolence that always hovered around the old man himself. "You *were* in Venice," I said suddenly. "That smell was in the train compartment. You must have put the book there yourself."

The light came on, a single dim bulb of about fifteen watts hanging from the center of the ceiling. "You see? Is modern, is convenience," he said, rubbing his hands.

The room was so crammed with junk that getting across it was a labyrinthine proposition. There was no straight path. No matter which way you went, you could take no more than two or three steps before being confronted by some obstacle. Everywhere there were crates and bookcases piled with yellowed newspapers and magazines or stacks of dirty dishes or heaps of clothes. There did seem to be a sofa and an armchair, each draped haphazardly with a variety of printed fabrics, but since they were both pressed tightly against the back of a large chest of drawers, it seemed unlikely that any human being could be agile enough to sit down on them. That was probably just as well. For as I watched, what I had first thought to be a lot of fuzzy little pillows began to squirm and stretch and nuzzle one another. A couple of the cats made their way over the chest of drawers and jumped down to rub against the old man's ankles.

"Where's Humphrey?"

"Huh?" The man was bending over very slowly to pet the animals. "Oh, yeh, I understand. Is brother, who write music."

"I have to make sure he's all right," I said, meaning, "I have to make sure he's really here."

"Yeh, sure, sure, I take you. But first I want show—"

"No. First I see Humphrey. Just tell me where he is."

The old man flapped his hand impatiently. "But he sleep! Is nothing to see, to say to him. And I want show—"

"Tell me where he is!"

"Oh, yeh, yeh, I take," he said irritably, pushed the cats away and tottered toward me. "Is up above. Follow."

The stairway was just opposite the door, so I did not have to thread my way across the room to reach it. I let the old man go first. I was burning with impatience now, but he took his time. The stairway was so steep that he literally had to crawl, pulling himself up with hands and feet, inch by trembling inch. At the top, we were again in complete darkness. With one hand against the wall, I followed what I thought was the gentle rasp of the old man's breathing—until it stopped.

"Hey, come on, let's keep going," I said, reaching forward to push him. Nothing was there.

"Hey, what's the matter? Where are you?" I blurted out. Then I shut up, to try to hear where he had gone. But the house itself made so many sighing and shuffling noises that I could not isolate his breathing, or even his footsteps. I began to panic and cursed my own stupidity. He didn't have Humphrey at all. He had lured me here, had put me into this helpless position, and was now going to stab or shoot me in the darkness to get revenge for what we had done. "Hey, come on! Say something!" I called hollowly. It occurred to me, as I waited for an answer, that the medicinal odor was more pronounced up here. There was no answer. Then I recognized the odor. It was formaldehyde, the chemical used for preserving dead things in bottles. He wasn't merely going to kill me. He was a maniac with a collection. After the murder he would can me in big glass Ball jars. Would the first jab of the knife be in my back or my stomach—or perhaps the side, just under my rib cage? As I thought of each location, the skin there began to itch. "Hey, where are you?" I called again. The hallway was miserably cold and damp, but I was sweating nonetheless. Probably the next thing I would feel would be a razor blade slicing through my jugular.

"Is bloody stupidness!" shrieked the old man from somewhere off to the left. There was the sound of shattering glass and then a low moan. I must have jumped about a foot. "Aha! Is find at last," he went on. A yellow light splashed across the wall, complete with the old man's bent, flickering shadow. There was a doorway just ahead of me on the left. I hurried through.

The old man was fussing with an oil lamp on a cluttered wooden table. In trying to find it in the darkness, he had knocked off some dirty teacups; I could see their fragments on the floor. More piles of old periodicals took up most of the space in the tiny room. There were many gaping wounds in the hideous flowered wallpaper, revealing the wooden lath underneath. A thin, grimy towel was tacked up over the one small window. Beneath the window, on a narrow and sagging institutional-type bed that could barely contain him, lay Humphrey, just waking up. "What's that noise?" he grunted.

In a moment I was kneeling beside the bed, awkwardly attempting to embrace him. "Humphrey," I said. "It's me, Sammy. I'm sorry, Humphrey, I'm so sorry."

He blinked his groggy little eyes and wiped his hand across his face. "Do you serve towels with your showers, Sam?" he said.

12

HE MUST have developed a slight tolerance to the
drug. Bridget had certainly dosed him often enough. But
the pill still had some effect. Humphrey was only half
awake, and definitely not his normal self.

I pulled away from him slightly. "But I mean it,
Humphrey," I said. "I truly am sorry about all the horrible things I've ever done, and especially about the way
I told you about what was happening. You didn't de-
serve it."

"I don't want to talk about it," he said, and yawned.

"Listen to me, Humphrey!" I screamed, shaking
him. "I love you. Do you hear me? I love you." The
shake had turned into another awkward embrace. "I love
you more than anything, Humphrey. Don't you understand?"

"Sure, Sam," he said, smacking his lips in a familiar,
irritating way. His eyelids began to slide shut. "You're
my brother. I'm supposed to love you, too."

I was appalled. Where was the passionate outpour-
ing of emotions I had imagined, the remorse, the tearful
explanations, and finally the forgiveness I craved? I felt

like a wanderer in the desert who had finally reached the distant oasis, my body poised in anticipation of the first life-saving drink. Humphrey was offering me the dry dust of a mirage. I squeezed his face between my two hands, forgetting about the old man. "But Humphrey, don't you even care? After what I told you about the whole thing being just a trick, remember? How I make up the Magyar pieces and then we drug you and just plant them? Don't you even want to know how I feel, how sorry I am? Don't you even want to tell me how *you* feel?"

"I tol' you, I don' wanna talk about it now," he mumbled, rolling over on the bed to face away from me. Whether it was the drug, or some kind of avoidance mechanism on his part, or a combination of both, the result was the same. I shook him, I slapped him, I pulled his hair. And he refused to be conscious.

Finally I pushed him away and stood up. I saw the filthy towel and smelled the formaldehyde, and the fact of where I was registered. But it seemed insignificant compared to the unsatisfied emotions that pierced me. I could have been an addict on withdrawal. The practical importance of what I had just done did not begin to dawn on me until, in the distance, I heard a voice say, "So is *you* who are composing and not Humpy at all."

"Huh?" I said slowly, turning around.

A funny-looking little old man stood in a wretchedly squalid room. "So is *you* who are composing the Magyar, yes?" he asked me through a big grin, lamplight glittering in his excited eyes.

"Oh, my God," I said, and sank down onto the bed.

What a pathetic ass I was! Even after the blow he'd received, Humphrey had resisted whatever urge he might have had to give us all away. And then I had stepped in and let the whole story gush hysterically out of me. "God, what a *dope!*" I said.

"But I no understand. You are compose the Magyar, yeh?"

On the other hand, why shouldn't I tell him? The scheme was finished now, I saw with relief—neither Humphrey nor I would be able to keep it up any longer. And probably the old guy had already been planning to expose us anyway. "But . . . oh, well, I guess it doesn't matter any more. Yeah, I'm the one who cranks out the crap," I told him. "The whole thing . . ." I gulped. "Well, it's just a fake. You must have known it was."

"Fake . . . I knew?" He was closer, leaning over me.

"Sure. If anybody could see it was phony, it would be you. You're the authority on his life and work, the writer of his biography; you knew everything about him." It was all falling into place now as I spoke. I hardly had to do any thinking at all. "I mean look." I gestured bleakly at the room. "You're his only son and obviously not making any money from his music. And then we come along with these fake concoctions and start raking in the cash. No wonder you followed us around; no wonder you said things to try to frighten us. Of course it was unfair, and you wanted to stop it. Well, now you don't have to. I stopped it for you."

"I . . . see," he said, his head maintaining that tremble of permanent assent, his eyes still excited. "So newspaper is wrong? My father no come to talk with one who compose?"

"Please," I said. "Don't rub it in. I already feel guilty enough about Humphrey and everything else."

"Ah, is too bad then." He rubbed his hands, gazing past me with a faraway look. "And I so anticipate to ask what he say about . . . oh, about so many things." He laughed. "Even about his . . . how you say? . . . oh, yes, about his love life on other side. I am so sure he mention that thing, yeh."

"Oh, come on!" I pleaded, and pushed myself up from the bed. "I understand how you must feel. You want to get revenge, to take it out on somebody. But it's not really my fault. Bridget made me do it. That's our mother, Bridget, you know."

"She *make* you do compose?"

"Yes. And I know that sounds like passing the buck, but it isn't really. I tried to get out of it. I didn't want to do it, but she's like . . . How can I describe it? She's like a force of nature or something. I mean once she makes up her mind, *no one* can stop her."

"Yeh. Is all very interest, how happen." He beckoned to me to follow him, turning to leave the room. "Come. I show."

I felt a curious reluctance. "But . . . but I should stay with Humphrey?"

"Why? He fine, he safe. He sleep. No can forgive you when he sleep. In morning when he wake, can forgive you then. Come."

Now I felt more foolish. He made my profound emotions sound so petty. I followed him, more to explain myself than for any other reason. "You have to understand how it was," I said, feeling a certain relief in letting it all pour out, even though he probably comprehended only half of what I was saying. "The whole thing was Bridget's idea. And until just a few hours ago, Humphrey didn't know anything. He thought it was real. There was a reason for that . . ."

I went on talking as I followed him up another ladderlike flight of stairs. I told him about Bridget's idea of fooling Humphrey and then being skeptical ourselves, in order to make the story less implausible. "And it worked," I said, as we reached the top and were confronted with darkness again: he couldn't climb holding the lamp, and I hadn't thought to bring it. "We even fooled the experts."

"Yeh, but if music no good, no fool nobody," he said, invisible ahead of me. "How you do that, make the music?"

"You mean you *liked* it? You didn't think it was . . . an insult to your father's name?"

"Yeh, yeh, sure I like." This floor had the same layout as the one below. I still couldn't see anything, but I sensed him turning off to the left and followed close behind. "So tell me," he said impatiently, making a lot of noise as he fumbled for another lamp. "How you do music, I ask you!"

The unexpected praise, and the darkness vibrating before my eyes, made me curiously lightheaded. Or perhaps it was the poisonous reek of formaldehyde, so strong now it was intoxicating. "I just *did* it!" I said gaily. It felt good to be recognized at last. "I just sat down and scribbled. I used some American folk tunes, the way he used Gypsy songs. And I put in sounds I heard around me, like weather sounds or traffic noises." I laughed. "Or people blowing their noses or going to the bath—"

Curses interrupted me as more breakable objects met the floor. He was amazingly clumsy; one would have thought he would be less inept at lighting the lamps, since he had to do it every day. "Ah, is here!" he said, and struck a match. The flame lit his face eerily from below; his eyes sparkled at me out of deep, shadowy pits. "Yeh, now I show." He chuckled and touched the wick.

For the first time it occurred to me to wonder just what it was he kept babbling about showing me. Some battered old trinkets of his father's no doubt. I wanted him to get it over with so I could go on bragging about my compositions. The wick flared.

"After the first one or two, I wasn't even trying to copy him," I said, as the room appeared. The style of the decor remained consistent: more junk blackened by the grime of decades, more tattered piles of books and papers, more peeling wallpaper and rags and crumbling plaster. Only here there was an old upright piano instead of a bed, its black enameled finish blistered and cracked. The top was littered with falling-apart volumes of music, except for the space occupied by a large cylindrical glass jar, sealed with a cork. The pale objects floating inside were obscured by a thick coat of dust on the glass. "Hey, what's in that jar?" I asked.

"I no understand," he mumbled without turning around, preoccupied with stacks of papers on a small desk.

"Forget it, I can look for myself," I said. I went over to the piano and rubbed some of the dust off the glass. Then I swallowed, hard. All of a sudden I was sitting down on the piano bench.

"Jesus Christ," I said, when I was able to talk. My voice was so weak that the old man didn't hear or respond. I went on sitting there and staring dumbly at the hands in the jar.

They were a uniform waxen beige color, except for the long black hairs that sprouted from the knuckles and undulated lazily in the formaldehyde. They seemed shrunken somehow, shriveled, and there was a little grime under the fingernails—Düsseldorf dirt? The skin hung in ragged wisps where they had been severed at the wrist, and a limp blood vessel protruded wormlike from one of them. But the most disturbing thing about them was the unusual bone structure, the broad flat palms, the long, widely-spaced fingers that thickened toward the first joint and then tapered curiously toward the nails. They could have been Humphrey's hands.

"I thought . . . In the book, you said they were lost," I said at last.

"What is lost?" Now he was poking around on his hands and knees in the mess underneath the desk.

"The hands! Magyar's hands, of course. Isn't that what you wanted to show me?"

"Oh, hands!" He smiled jovially up at me. "Is interesting, yeh?"

"I thought you said they had been lost."

"Oh, no, no." He flapped his hand as though dismissing a foolish question. "That just story I make up. I like make up stories. I tell them. They believe. But what really happen . . ." He gave me a conspiratorial wink. "I take. But why let world know I take? Keep secret, yeh?"

"What about the . . . the head? Is that just a story, too?"

"No. Damn Sister got," he said heatedly. "She come say God tell her; they give. Not give to me. Me not big importance. Damn Sister take. So I put in book. Many people go perhaps see, make nuisance at bloody convent." He shrugged and went back to his search.

What did he want with these grisly relics? And if he had simply invented the story about the missing hands, then how much else in the book was invented? "Your father's hands," I said. "They look just like Humphrey's hands."

"Huh?" he said from the floor.

"The hands, they look just like Humphrey's!" I repeated. "I've never seen any other hands shaped like that."

"Aha, yeh, this I notice when Humpy write in program," he said, not turning around. "I tell you that before. Is interesting, yeh?"

I was beginning to be irritated by his preoccupation with the floor. "What are you doing, anyway?" I demanded.

"Is what I want show," he said. "I search to find."

I stood up. "Isn't that what you wanted to show me?" I cried, waving at the hands.

"Aha, is here, at last long," he said, and slowly struggled to his feet, beaming, an ancient leather satchel clasped to his chest.

"Who says I want to see any more?" I muttered. "Maybe I've seen enough already." The hands had been a shock. I didn't like the way the dead things resembled Humphrey's hands. I didn't like this cold and filthy house. I didn't like the old man's unpredictability. Instead of clearing up my problems, he was only making everything more confusing.

Now he was searching through the drawers of the desk. "Is key, I know somewhere is key," he murmured. The satchel had an old metal lock on it, I noticed.

"What is this thing you want to show me, anyway?"

"Aha, is interesting, yeh. You see."

At least I could assure myself that it wasn't going to be Magyar's head. Even if the story about the convent was a lie, there was no cranial bulge in that satchel.

I might have considered getting Humphrey and myself away from the old lunatic immediately, except that it was too much trouble to try to figure out where we would go when we left the house. I wondered vaguely about Bridget and Luc and looked at my watch. It was one-thirty. I tried to imagine what they were doing at this moment and couldn't. Their predicament might have been amusing, only they seemed so terribly distant from me—probably because I assumed that they would never be able to find us here . . .

"Aha, is key! Now I show." He could have been a genial Christmas gnome chortling over some marvelous toy. His hands trembling, he struggled with the lock. There seemed to be absolutely nothing of a mechanical nature that he didn't have trouble with. He tried the key one way and then the other; he pulled and jiggled the clasp; he swore and he drooled and finally he handed the thing to me.

"I'm no good with locks either," I said. But at least I knew enough to set the satchel down on the desk before trying to open it. The problem was that the lock and key were both so rusty. "This thing hasn't been opened in years," I said.

He shrugged. "No need. I know is there."

In the unlikely event that there was something valuable here, it would have been safe, camouflaged by all the obviously worthless junk. "But it's impossible!" I said after a few minutes. "Just tell me what's in it."

"No, must to see." He jittered and twitched beside me like a nervous bird, the breath whistling in his throat.

"But it won't open, dammit!"

"Yeh! Must open! Must try!"

Why was I letting him force me to do this pointless thing? Here I was in the middle of the biggest crisis in my life, trying to break open a package of old letters written in Hungarian, or something else equally thrilling. I jabbed at the key, tugged furiously, and suddenly the strap scraped out of the lock with an explosion of dust. "Here, dammit!" I said, coughing as I thrust it at him.

"No, no you! Is you do it!" His hands were quivering too spasmodically now to hold onto anything. The grin made a relief map out of his cheeks and turned his eyes into hairline slits.

I reached into the satchel. Even before pulling them out, I could sense the age of the papers inside. They felt almost as thin and fragile as newspaper ash. I lay them carefully on the desk. They were yellow in the lamplight, the edges cracked and crumbling away like powder. The blotched and scribbled musical notation had faded almost—but not quite—to the point of illegibility.

"Well? What is it?" I said, turning to him.

"Only look! Must look careful!"

I looked.

The room faded away, the old man, the house itself, Vienna, even Humphrey faded. One by one I turned over the sheets. And awe boomed around me, a great bell whose vibrations entered my bones from within the earth.

"When . . . ?" I said.

"In last month of life, before go to Düsseldorf. I keep; I save; No one see; no one know exist. Is never publish."

There were, of course, the few notes Luc had made me change. But except for those discrepancies, this music and my own compositions were absolutely the same.

13

THE NOTES before me, and the sensation of awe, these I could perceive with perfect clarity. Everything else was a mess. Was I disappointed, because in some inexplicable way I really hadn't written my music after all? Or was I elated for having been the medium through which this supernatural mystery had been accomplished? I didn't know. All I knew was that the music was the same, that my own hands had diligently reproduced these secret, unpublished scores. I looked at the stubby little fingers that I had always hated. I had the uncanny feeling that they didn't really belong to me at all, and at any moment might decide to crawl away and never return.

"Is interesting, yeh?" He gazed at me with an expression of bliss, awaiting my response like a puppy eager to be stroked.

I cleared my throat. "Yeah, well, at least nobody can say I didn't do a good job of imitating a certain dead composer," I feebly cracked.

"What? I no understand."

I didn't bother to explain. It occurred to me briefly

that it might be a trick. I suppose it was remotely possible that after hearing Humphrey perform the first three pieces he could have written them out by memory and somehow made them look old. But Humphrey had never performed the rest of the music, which had been composed for the Vienna concerts. The old man had never heard it. "But what does it mean?" I said.

"Who knows what mean? Only is humor, yeh? You think to fake my father. Only happen that is maybe no fake after all, yeh?"

"Yes, but . . . It wasn't as though I went into a trance or anything. It wasn't like automatic writing or speaking in tongues. I was conscious the whole time; I was *aware* of deciding what notes to write. At a seance the medium is supposed to pass out and not know what she does."

"Peh!" he expostulated with a grimace of contempt. "Seance is fake, is act. This real, yeh?"

"I don't *know.*" I was beginning to feel rather desperate. I turned back to the music. I knew I had never seen it or heard it. How could I have? Yet how could I have reproduced it so perfectly? I wasn't prepared to start believing in ghosts at a moment's notice.

"But what about you?" I said, turning back to the old man. "What did you *think* when Humphrey started playing this stuff?"

"I?" He thoughtfully scratched his scabby head. "Hard remember now . . ."

"In Venice. What did you think in Venice?"

"Huh? In Venice . . . Oh, yeh, yeh. I go concert; Humpy play like pig, then say he play piece by my father, new piece. Yeh, I am angry, think then fake, of course, to use, unfair. Then he play. Music is same. For one minute, I think Humpy steal somehow from here." He patted the satchel. "But yet, I know is not so. No one can look, no one know is unpublished music ever at all. I great confused, angry and mean and lost. Then I see in newspaper. Is boy talk about ghost. Then not mad, is very big interest. I follow."

"Naturally you would." Confusion and fear, as ever, were making me angry. "And you gave us little presents, like the book and the doll's hands, right?"

He smiled coyly, twisting his hands. "Yeh. Why not?"

"And gave us little hints, after the concerts. Except nobody heard them but me. Did you know that?"

"Well. Is most important for you hear, yeh?" He stuck out his chin and raised his eyebrows.

"Yes, and scared me half to death and made me a complete laughingstock. Do you realize how . . . foolish and pitiful it all made me feel? What a dope? Nobody believed me! Why didn't you just come out and *tell* us, all of us? Why didn't you just *produce* this music?"

He grabbed my hand with both of his and squeezed. There was unexpected strength in those arthritic old bones. "Yeh, I want, but then I think. For once, I think. For once in life, I do right thing," he said with fervor. "If show, then end everything. What is happening, it will stop. If I show, then we never know. And now I ask . . ." He brought his face close to mine, spraying me delicately with spittle. "Is other pieces you write, after those I hear? Is same, yeh?"

"Yes, yes, they're the same, all four of them!" I said, pulling my hand away from him. He was right not to tell us any earlier, of course. It would have been unthinkably stupid to interfere with the process. But that didn't make me any less angry. I felt somehow more taken advantage of than ever.

"Ah, yeh, yeh, I knew would be same," he said happily.

"I'm glad you're getting such a kick out of it," I said. "But it sure wasn't a whole lot of fun for me. That bundle on Humphrey's bed, that was a real nasty jolt. What did you do, bribe the chambermaid?"

"Oh, yeh, Elsa, easy. You like?"

"Sure, I loved it; it was cuter than hell," I said. "Is that what your father had inside his bundle? A pair of doll's hands?"

"Oh, no, no, father have no such bundle," he said, shaking his head. "That only another story I make up, for fun, to be interest in book. Nice touch, eh?"

For a moment I wanted to kick him. Then something hit me. "Hey, wait a minute," I said. "The hands. Humphrey *predicted* that! He knew the hands were going to appear."

"No! How Humpy know that?" He sounded just as amazed as I did.

"I don't know. But he knew other things, too. And the way he played the—"

But before I had a chance to go on there came a terrible bleating buzz in D Flat, more painful than the most penetrating of alarm clocks. I emitted a doglike yelp. "What was that?" I cried out, my heart suddenly thumping a kettledrum tattoo.

He was already tottering toward the window. "Is
. . . how you say? . . . Is door . . ."

"Oh, no!" I was there beside him. He was struggling to get the window open, to look down and see who
it was. He couldn't make it budge, of course. "Wait!
Stop!" I said. "Don't let them know we're here!"

"Must see who is!" he grunted, and with heroic
effort he shoved open the window, which emitted a
piercing squeal. We leaned out. Bridget and Luc, illu-
minated by the headlights of a taxi that was waiting in
the alley, heard the window and looked up. It was impossible to tell if they could see us or not.

"Don't let them in!" I whispered frantically, pulling him back into the room. "Maybe they didn't see us."

"Okeh, okeh," he muttered. "But . . ."

Then I distinctly heard the front door open and
shut and footsteps in the downstairs hall.

"But how did they get in?" I growled, squeezing his
scrawny shoulders.

"Ah!" He struck his forehead with his hand and
grinned sheepishly. "Is stupid me." He chuckled. "Never
I can remember lock door."

14

ONLY THE IMAGE of those brittle bones shattering like his old teacups kept me from dashing him to the floor.

I was totally unprepared to face Bridget and Luc. And then I thought of Humphrey. I couldn't let them take Humphrey away from me now. I had to get to him first. "Hide us, you must hide us!" I whispered. I dragged the old man after me into the hall.

He choked and whimpered something about the music, but I was ruthless. At the stairway I hoisted him onto my rump, feeling the sharp pelvic bones under the empty flesh of his buttocks, and started blindly down. I stumbled and slipped sickeningly, careening into the banister, but by some miracle landed at the bottom on my feet.

The sight of Magyar's hands had been a delightful joke compared to the horror of hearing Bridget's voice hoarsely calling our names. They were still on the first floor, but it would be only moments before the noise I was making brought them up to us. Still lugging the old man I lurched toward the bedroom, crashing into the wall before making it through the doorway. The lamp sputtered dimly. Humphrey was sitting up in bed, his mouth opening to answer Bridget.

I raced to the bed and covered his mouth with my hand, letting go of the old man in the process. He saved himself from falling to the floor by clinging to my neck with jagged fingernails. "Shhhh! Don't answer, Humphrey!" I croaked. "They mustn't find us!"

Humphrey's lips writhed, his furiously expelled breath making wet noises against the skin of my hand as he struggled to speak.

"Come on, Luc, they're upstairs!" said Bridget.

"But . . . but what if . . . ?"

"Just come *on!*" One of them bumped into a piece of furniture, and then there were the first careful footsteps on the stairs.

"Listen to me, Humphrey!" I pleaded. "You've got to believe me. It's true after all! I *mean* it! Everything's changed. That music really did come from Magyar. There's proof, real physical proof. Bridget will destroy it if she finds out!"

He was grinding my skin beneath his teeth now. The old man was still digging his fingers into my neck.

"Trust me, Humphrey! This one last time, just please, *please* trust me now. It's our last chance to—"

Humphrey's body was a weak pile of flab, but for two major exceptions. Now he took hold of my wrist with his powerful hands and twisted. I bellowed in agony and wrenched myself away from him, knocking his head back against the window. The old man saved himself from being trampled as I staggered backwards by flinging himself onto the bed with perfect timing. My feet slid into a pile of books and my coccyx hit the floor.

"We're upstairs! Sam's hurting me!" Humphrey screamed unnecessarily as Bridget and Luc plunged into the room. The towel over the window was draped around Humphrey's face like a grimy bridal veil, the old man nestled kittenlike against his belly, and I reclined amid scattered volumes on the floor.

No one spoke. A couple of cats from downstairs came padding over to sniff at my face. I shoved them rudely away. My backbone was killing me. I pushed myself up to a sitting position. The old man uncurled himself from Humphrey and struggled to his feet. Humphrey pushed the towel away from his face.

"What in hell is going on here?" Bridget said at last.

"Sam was *hurting* me," Humphrey whined.

"Oh, my poor baby!" Bridget rushed over to the bed, knelt beside him, and began stroking his hair. "What happened to you? Are you all right, sweetheart?"

"I feel funny," Humphrey said, sniffling.

"It's only the drug," I said, standing up and rubbing my rear end. "He's been treated fine."

Then Luc had my hands pinned behind my back. "He'd better be all right, you little swine," he said. "What have you done to him? Tell us!"

"Get your fat hands off me!" I twisted away from him, knocking over another pile of books. "You might as well stop pushing me around, it's too late now." I gestured at the little old man. "Don't you want to meet our host?"

They both looked at him as if they hadn't noticed him before. He was adjusting his frayed lapels with an attempt at dignity, regarding them staunchly. "Allow me," he began, with a stiff little bow. "I am—"

"What the hell is this place, anyway?" Bridget interrupted, turning away from him. "How did you and Humphrey both get here?"

"If you'd listen to him, you might figure it out," I said. "Don't you even recognize him?"

But his appearance was too unprepossessing to be of any interest to Bridget. She barely gave him a second glance. "Answer my question, Sam!" she demanded.

But Humphrey was watching him. "I think I . . . I remember him. He was the one . . . He was nice to me, when I ran away, before I woke up here. I think he helped me. He told me something." Even though Humphrey dwarfed Bridget on the little bed, he was managing to snuggle up against her. "Who is he, Mama?"

Now Luc was studying the old man as well, adjusting his glasses. "Yes, Sam. Who is he?" he said uncomfortably. "There's something . . ."

"Why don't you let him tell you himself?" I said. "I've already mentioned him oodles of times."

"Well?" Bridget asked him rudely.

The old man seemed dejected now, for the first time since I had laid eyes on him. He watched me, not them, as he spoke. "My name," he said sadly, "my name, is Laszlo Magyar."

Bridget's snort was highly unladylike. "Very funny," she said.

"Wait a minute . . ." said Luc.

Bridget ignored him. "We have no time for games," she said, patting Humphrey's shoulder and pulling away from him. "Now we have to get Humphrey back to the hotel and get him rested up. Later on we can find out how you both got to this dump."

"Oh, you dope, you *dope!*" I wailed, stamping my foot. "Can't you pay attention for *once?* He's not Magyar, of *course* he's not! He's his son; he's been following us around; I kept trying to tell you!"

"My God!" said Luc, starting toward him and then quickly backing away. "There is—there is a resemblance." He turned to Bridget. "There really is."

Magyar had died at fifty, and Laszlo junior was a good thirty years older than that. Yet his high forehead and beaky nose could have been lifted from the portrait in the front of the book. If I had noticed it before, it hadn't been consciously. Now I could see that the resemblance was unmistakable.

But Bridget had hardly bothered to glance at the book—that wasn't her part of the operation. She stood up. "Don't be a fool, Luc. It's all Sam's sick imagination. The guy's just an old bum."

"But . . . he could be," Luc said, shaking his head. "The resemblance . . . it's amazing."

"I don't care who the hell he says he is," Bridget said, still denying Laszlo the courtesy of addressing him directly. "We have a big day tomorrow, and Humphrey has to have some rest. And that cab waiting out there is costing us a fortune."

She was on her way again, with that concentrated, headlong energy. Once again I had underestimated her, imagining the events of the night to be a hurdle even she couldn't jump. I had simply assumed that she would have to give up now and stop pushing Humphrey.

But she hadn't experienced what I had. The situation had no more credibility for her than all the other elephants I had dropped in her path. She was stepping easily over the carcass as though it were a squashed ant. And I couldn't stand it. The urge I felt to stop her once and for all was uncontrollable, beyond safety or reason, the culmination of eighteen crippling years. And now I *had* the chance to stop her and save Humphrey from her—it was my last chance.

"Come on, Humphrey," she said, pulling away the rank bedclothes with an expression of disgust. "Time to go home to sleep."

"But Mama, what if he really is?" said Humphrey.

"It doesn't matter who he is, she doesn't care about that," I said. "But she might be interested to find out how much he knows."

She spun around. "What's that supposed to mean?"

"Give up, Bridget. He knows everything. Humphrey's career is over, no matter how much you go on browbeating us. Because you can't stop him from going to the press. I told him the whole story."

"Do you mean that, Sam?" she said, her face blank. There was no reason to answer; she knew I was telling the truth. She turned to Laszlo then, appraising him carefully for the first time—his age, his apparent poverty, his trembling weakness. Then his eyes wavered and he looked shamefacedly down.

"Tell her!" I begged him. "Tell her you know the

whole thing's a hoax, that Magyar's ghost is a fake. Tell her you're going to the papers tomorrow!"

"Excuse pliz . . . but, but . . ." he said. What was the matter with him? "But is no fake, yeh? I know music is real."

Bridget laughed. It was a sound I hadn't heard from her in years, a real laugh, full and abandoned.

"Is no fake," he insisted, clenching his fists. "I show. I prove."

"No!" I shrieked. "No! Don't!"

"Don't what?" Bridget said, really interested now. She approached Laszlo. "Prove what?"

"I have, yeh, yeh, I have," he said, drooling with excitement. "I have real proof, to touch, to hold, to show press. Prove is truly Magyar's music from boy. Come. I show."

But he was wrong. Yeh, to those of us in this room, the music upstairs was proof of the supernatural. But to everyone else in the world it would be proof only of our hoax. It could be demonstrated scientifically that those manuscripts had been written by Magyar years before Humphrey had performed his first new Magyar composition. After that, there would be no doubt in anyone's mind that our ghost was phony. The music was there. Not even the most fervent spiritualist would believe that we hadn't worked together and plotted the whole thing out, that we hadn't merely copied the originals. The irony was magnificent: The only real evidence of the music's supernatural origin was at the same time the one tangible document that would show Humphrey to be a fake.

I still didn't know how I felt about the music, or

what it meant about my talents. In another, prettier life it would have been marvelous to explore the significance of it, to share with the rest of the world this incredible thing that had happened to *me*. But in our situation, the manuscripts had another function that was far more important. To display the manuscripts and confess to having copied them would stop Bridget for good and save us from her once and for all. After that, she would never be able to push Humphrey out on stage again.

And Bridget would know all that, the instant she got a glimpse of the music.

"Come. I show," said Laszlo, starting for the hall. "Is upstairs."

"She'll destroy it, you idiot!" I bellowed. "Don't you *understand?*" I grabbed his coattails and pulled him away from the door.

"Luc. Humphrey. Get him," ordered Bridget.

I fought like a wildman, but I was no match for the two of them. In a moment they were both sitting on me.

"Oh, Laszlo, don't you see, don't you see what she is?" I wept. "She'll destroy it, she will, she will, she will . . ."

He watched me curiously.

"Come on, show me," Bridget said.

"But I want to see it, too," said Luc.

"Me, too," said Humphrey.

"Then I'm afraid you'll have to find some way to keep Sam under control," said Bridget from the door. "Knock him out or something."

"But . . . how?" Luc wondered, kneeling across my thighs.

Humphrey, straddling my chest, didn't need to ask. I saw his big malformed fist come swinging down toward the side of my head. Then I didn't see anything for a while.

15

THE VOICES seemed to be coming from a great distance, calling my name. My head hurt. I groaned. I knew there was some urgent reason to wake up, only my eyes didn't want to move.

But consciousness trickled slowly back, and with it came the miserable awareness of what had just happened. Then I smelled smoke. At that point, I saw no reason to open my eyes at all.

A cold and slimy liquid splashed across my face—stale sugary tea. It was disgustingly sticky. I blinked, lifted my head and tried to wipe it away. Humphrey and Laszlo loomed over me. The world was blurred, but I could see the tears on Humphrey's cheeks.

"Sam, wake up, wake up, they're burning the music!" he wailed.

"Do you serve towels with your showers, Humphrey?" I said.

"But Sam! That music proves *you're* the special one, the one with Magyar's ghost!"

"Here. Drink," Laszlo said. He extended an ancient bottle toward me. It didn't smell like formaldehyde. I drank.

I yelped and sat up, almost knocking him over. "What's *that?*" —

"Is brandy from plum pit. Very special."

"Sam, they're burning it!" Humphrey said.

"What the hell did you *expect* them to do?" I said, rubbing my head. "You didn't have to hit me so hard."

"But now no one will ever believe what really happened," Humphrey whimpered. "Or how special you are."

"No, you've got it all wrong. You're both wrong, you dumb jerks." Anger at their stupidity was taking the fuzziness away. "Anyone who saw that music would think I just copied it. It's the only logical explanation. Think about it. It would make them *stop* believing." My head throbbed, and I groaned. "Then Bridget would have to stop pushing you, Humphrey. You wouldn't have to perform all the time. You could do whatever you wanted. But *now* she can go pushing us around forever. That's why she's burning it. Get it? Everything's . . . Oh, God . . . It's just going to be the same."

"You mean . . . you would lie about what happened, about the music, tell them it was fake, just to help *me?*"

"I might have."

Laszlo drank deeply from the bottle and smacked his lips. "Good stuff all right," he said.

"Damn you!" I snarled at him. "Why did you . . ." But then I felt too hopeless to go on being angry. "Oh well, I guess you didn't know. How could anybody know what she's like? I never had a chance to tell you."

Laszlo took another snort and corked the bottle. "Come, we go now," he said.

"But Mama and Papa . . ." Humphrey was bewildered. "How can they burn it? They can do *that*? They don't even *care* what it means?"

"Yeah, they can do that, Humphrey. Don't you know them by now?"

"Come, we go, must go," Laszlo said more urgently. "They finish soon."

"Go where?" I said. "What difference does it make?"

"Is that why you told me everything? To try to stop them from using me?" Humphrey said, screwing up his face as he puzzled it out.

The brandy had made me a little drunk, and it seemed too difficult at this moment to say anything but the truth. "I mostly did it to hurt you. I was jealous, like you said. But also, yes, I couldn't stand the whole thing any more. I thought that was the way to stop it. What a laugh."

Laszlo tugged at my shoulder. "Pliz, must go, fast, go quiet and fast." What was he afraid of, anyway?

"But how could they just go on *lying* to me that way?" Humphrey said woefully. "And you stopped lying, Sammy . . ."

My feelings for him always seemed to emerge at the oddest moments. With one arm I weakly embraced him. "I'm sorry, Humphrey. I wish I'd never been a part of it. It's rough. They're . . . But I care about you, I love you, anyway. I know it sounds funny, but I do. Whatever that's worth."

"You told me, you told me." The tears made Humphrey's eyes unaccountably beautiful. "You did want to stop it. You were the only one who cared."

"Yeah, but you *liked* it, Humphrey. For you, it was fun."

"Sort of, at first. But then it got different. I didn't even know how much I hated it." He looked up at the ceiling. We could hear footsteps and voices. There seemed to be wisps of smoke drifting through the cracks between the boards. "They . . . how *can* they? Now no one will believe you."

"Come, come we go! Pick him up, Humpy. Is more important than you know!"

I didn't relish the idea of staying to witness Bridget's triumph. "Oh, all right, all right," I said. Humphrey gently helped me to my feet. A fact was coming back to me that had only begun to assume importance in the moment before Bridget and Luc had arrived. "But Humphrey, you know what? I think maybe you're special, too, I think—"

"Yeh, yeh, yeh, outside." Laszlo was twitching around now in an agony of impatience. "Is more to tell! Must get outside now!"

My legs were shaky. Humphrey helped me down the stairs. We were even slower than Laszlo, who waited for us, hopping, at the front door. He pushed us out, then turned back to lock the door carefully. "Will be time before they get out," he said. "Come."

In the alley their cab was still waiting, which seemed amazing until we saw that the driver had fallen asleep. "Quick, inside," said Laszlo.

"We don't have any money," I informed him.

"Is no problem, money. Inside."

"Don't tell me you have enough to pay for a cab!"

"I pay. We go."

I didn't believe him but saw no reason to refuse. We crawled in. Laszlo nudged the driver until he jerked awake, then babbled at him in German. The car shuddered and lurched down the alley.

After several sharp turns, Laszlo stopped looking behind and sank back into the seat, rubbing his hands and cackling.

"You're taking this whole thing very lightly," I said, bothered by his good humor. Didn't he care about the music?

"Is adventure, yeh?" he said.

I couldn't figure out what was the matter with him. "Sure, until they find us again. You said you had more to tell. So out with it."

"Aha, yeh." He took hold of Humphrey's hands. "And how you feel, when you play Laszlo Magyar music, yeh, Humpy?"

"Huh?" said Humphrey stupidly.

"Oh, that's right." It was the fact I hadn't had a chance to mention, back in the house: The unexpected artistry with which Humphrey had performed the Magyar pieces. "You played that music really well, Humphrey. It was the only music you ever played like a musician."

"Yeh, yeh! How you feel when play?" said Laszlo, bouncing up and down on the seat.

"Well, I . . ." We passed a streetlight, and I saw Humphrey's brow wrinkle the way it did when he was thinking hard.

"Did you feel different than when you play Bach?" I asked him. My interest was purely theoretical; it was too late for the truth, however miraculous, to make much difference.

"Oh, yeah," Humphrey said. "I guess I didn't think about it; I just did it. Everything else I played, I thought about it all the time. But that music I didn't worry about . . . about Papa, or anything. I just had fun with it."

Laszlo clapped his hands. "See? See? Is influence here too, yeh? This also we explore."

"What the hell are you talking about?" His meaningless enthusiasm only made me more bitter.

"We three. We go together, away from them. Work for ourselves, together. No make concert. We explore. We learn. We solve deep mystery."

"Oh, stop it! You're just making it worse." Of course I had considered running away many times, but Bridget had always squashed that idea. Humphrey and I had no money, we had no way of earning money without them, unless we wanted to dig ditches or wait on tables, as Bridget frequently pointed out. The only realistic thing to do was go back and keep playing along with their filthy scheme, soul-destroying though it was. "We can't go away, and we'll never solve any mystery," I said. "We don't have anywhere to go, or any money, or anything." I was feeling more miserable by the minute. "This dumb cab ride that we can't pay for is the whole adventure." I looked dully out the window. "Where are you taking us, anyway?"

"To train, to boat," he said gleefully.

He must have really flipped his lid. "Come off it. Who's going to pay? We have nothing, and you don't even have enough to buy a new pair of pants."

189

His laughter now had the same abandon as Bridget's, only it wasn't proud and triumphant, it was warm and full of fun. I shrank back against the door and scowled at him. He really was a lunatic after all.

The thought of going back to Bridget made me want to curl up and die. But what else was there to do? Even if I ran away, what would I do with Humphrey? Rotten as it was for him to be with Bridget and Luc, it was probably better than living homelessly from hand to mouth with me.

"Who wants new pants? Why waste money on pants? I have plenty money for important things," Laszlo cried. "How you think I travel around, follow you? Money from father, of course. How you say? Ah yeh. Royalties! Inheritances. And now we make more money, by sell music. Music I been saving long, long time for . . . How you say? . . . Oh, yes, for rain of day."

"*Now* what are you talking about?"

"Last compositions of father, last seven compositions, yeh? Very valuable."

Now I saw what effect their crime had had on him. The loss of that precious music had made him mad. "They burned it up, don't you remember?" I said cruelly. "It's gone, forever."

"No, no, only copy. They burn copy."

"*What?*" Humphrey and I cried.

"You think I stupid, leave precious music there, in house in town? Oh, no, no." He wagged his finger at me engagingly. "Maybe person can break in and steal. Oh, no. I write out copy, soon as he die. I keep copy, have with me. That my writing, not his."

"You mean you have the originals somewhere else?" I was still refusing to let it sink in.

"Yeh, yeh, of course. I save for day of rain. In safe place, very very safe place, no one find ever."

I glanced at Humphrey as we both bent over the old man. Humphrey was looking at me in a new way, as though I were an equal, neither better nor worse than him. The electric excitement that crackled between us was more than a physical sensation; I felt as though I were really waking up for the first time in my life. "Where?" I said with difficulty. "Where is the music?"

"Wonderful safe place, inherit from father. My father leave me house, money, but also leave me another place, secret place. Is safe there, music. Is safe on island."

16

NOW WE ARE on the island.

It's a small island, a rocky meadow pushed up out of the Danube like the last ragged squirt of a giant toothpaste tube. The endlessness of water and sky is everywhere around us, and the wind. Nothing crowds in on us at all. Humphrey says it's a lot like the island in his dream. I haven't gotten around to thinking much about that.

Actually the most dreamlike thing about the place is the house, which Magyar had built to look like a miniature gothic ruin. The arched hall and the two little towers aren't particularly cozy. But that couldn't matter less—Magyar's stolen Bösendorfer grand is still in excellent condition.

It's been almost four months since Laszlo brought us here, picked up the scores, and then went off to arrange a fast, lucrative deal with his father's German publisher. The publicity Humphrey had achieved only added to the value of the music, of course. Laszlo let the publisher handle the press, but waited around just long enough to collect a good sample of the results. Then he rushed back to us with the papers, as well as several cases of Coke and a few other necessities.

It was a curious experience to sit in the little gazebo on the water's edge and read about Laszlo's fraudulent plot—and Bridget and Luc's complicity, of course. Humphrey, being a malleable child, escaped much of the blame, and I was barely mentioned at all. Laszlo was accused of sullying his father's name by using Humphrey to boost the value of the scores he had been planning to release all along. Bridget and Luc were censured for involving their child in this sordid scheme. But their treatment was mild compared to what they would have received if we'd told more of the details. Bridget knew they were getting off easy. She made no counterattacks, no denials, only "no comment." After the publisher produced the authenticated scores, accompanied by Laszlo's confession of the "arrangement" he had made with her, what else could she say? That we had somehow innocently come up with the music ourselves, without knowing of the scores' existence? She knew no one would fall for an alibi so fantastic and pitifully transparent.

The helplessness of her position must have been frustrating for her to say the least, and I wondered how she was taking it out on poor Luc. I also wondered about her own interpretation of the events. Once she had taken the immediate practical measure of burning the copies, had she ever allowed the fact to sink in that they were real evidence of the supernatural? Or was that phenomenon just another messy elephant to be made invisible by the power of her will?

Humphrey, certainly, was plagued by the irony of

the situation. Having been gifted by the supernatural, I was now sitting by and allowing the world to dismiss it as a commonplace case of fraud. He saw it as a tremendous sacrifice that I had made in order to rescue him. He couldn't get over it at first and wouldn't stop talking about the unfairness of life. Unlike me, the past hadn't conditioned him to accept injustice.

I finally calmed him down by promising that we would tell the real story eventually, that someday we would get in touch with Nitpikskaya, perhaps even offer ourselves as subjects at the institute in Moscow. We had plenty of time for all that; we would never lose the knowledge of what had happened to us. What mattered most at the moment was that Laszlo had gotten the money from the music quickly—without trying to make any supernatural claims about it—and Bridget had been exposed. Best of all, by releasing the music as we had, we had put a stop to Humphrey's performing. As I had hoped, the scandal had wrecked his career for the time being. Even if Bridget should find out where we were hiding, it was too late for her to put him back on the concert platform.

Neither of us wanted to be with Bridget and Luc. Humphrey had been hurt badly by the knowledge of how they had duped him and made use of him. Then, to see them cold-bloodedly burn that music had been enough to blacken whatever good feelings were left. It was painful for him just to think about them, let alone go back to live with them. They had taken so much from both of us that now we had nothing left to give them, and certainly they had nothing to offer us any more. All they could do was interfere with our mutual healing process. Perhaps at some time in the future we would recover enough to face them again, but for the time being they had severed the bonds between us as completely as the trolley wheels had severed Magyar's head and hands.

I was eighteen and legally free of them, but Humphrey wasn't. By law, they could get him back—if they could find him. Fritz at the hotel had told them how to get to Laszlo's house, but the island was another matter. It had been Magyar senior's secret retreat in the last century; even then, hardly anyone had known of its existence. Now only Laszlo and a handful of dour river boatmen could locate the place. These he paid enough to bring us the supplies we needed and to keep their mouths shut. Even the publishers didn't know about the island, but they had told the press, at Laszlo's instruction, that Humphrey and I were safe and well. Bridget and Luc know we're all right, and that's about as much as we feel we owe them.

Now that we've had a chance to calm down, things are really pretty nice. There's so much space here, and Laszlo seems genuinely thrilled to have us. He never married or had any children, and he claims this is the first time in years that he hasn't been lonely. Certainly he couldn't find a more receptive audience for his stories about his father, which he can tell by the hour. It seems that Magyar was hardly an ideal parent himself, by the way. His attachment to his son was as sporadic as his interest in his various lovers. But he did, at least, leave him the royalties from his music, as well as the house in Vienna, the island, and those last seven compositions.

And Laszlo adores him. He's even beginning to write another book about him.

When he isn't working with Humphrey, that is. Like me, he could never play very well, but he's a wonderful teacher and has trained several successful pianists. Now that Humphrey doesn't have to worry about giving concerts all the time, his playing is improving enormously. Already he sounds like another person—or like the person he was when he performed those Magyar pieces.

And I'm composing. It doesn't come as easily as it did when I was trying to imitate Magyar, in fact it's a tremendous struggle. Sometimes it takes me all day to write one page. But I keep plugging away at it. There really isn't much else to do here, except go for walks around the island, or have picnics in the meadow, or gaze out over the river, or just sit around gabbing with Laszlo and with Humphrey. It turns out that Humphrey isn't so stupid after all. His backwardness must have had something to do with the way Luc and Bridget kept him chained to the piano and never gave him a chance to learn anything else. There are a lot of books in English here and he's beginning to read them, and he comes up with the most amazing insights sometimes. It doesn't even bore me to be stuck here with him. The feeling for him that broke over me on the night we ran away is stronger than ever now. I guess it must have been there all the time, buried under all the jealousy and resentment. And maudlin as it sounds, I think I'm beginning to love Laszlo, too.

He calls us his family. He might be right—in more ways than one. I still don't understand what happened

when we were involved in the hoax. I've thought of
mental telepathy and all sorts of things. But I had the
strangest idea of all the other day. It has to do with the
way Magyar died, having his hands and his head separated. Maybe his spirit came back in two parts, and I
got the head and Humphrey got the hands. That way,
the two of us together would be, in a way, the reincarna-
tion of one person: I write the music, and Humphrey
plays it. He always did play my music better than anything else.

That might explain the weird thing that happened
last night. It scares me a little to think about it. Neither
of us is really comfortable in our bedroom in the tower,
and last night we both had nightmares again. I can't remember my dream, and Humphrey can't remember his,
but we woke each other up at the same time, talking in
our sleep.

In Hungarian, Laszlo told us.